TEACHING TECHNIQUES

TEACHING TECHNIQUES

Becoming an Effective Teacher

KEN RIGGS

EVANGELICAL TRAINING ASSOCIATION
P.O. Box 327, Wheaton, IL 60189-327

Teaching Techniques, Becoming An Effective Teacher

All Scripture quotations are taken from The King James Version Bible.

ISBN: 978-1-929852-40-6

Printed in the United States of America

Cover Design: Chris Ward, UMI.

Contents

INTRODUCTION

In 1935, Dr. Clarence H. Benson, a professor at Moody Bible Institute and founder of Evangelical Training Association (ETA), published *Teaching Techniques*, one of the first books used to train Christian teachers. Since that time, more than 500,000 copies have been distributed. *Understanding Teaching*, written by Dr. Kenneth O. Gangel, was published in 1968 to replace Dr. Benson's original book. In 1998, *Understanding Teaching: Effective Biblical Teaching for the 21st Century*, written by Dr. Gregory C. Carlson, was published for the purpose of serving as the foundational ETA course in teacher training. In 2001, ETA published *Teaching Techniques: Revitalizing Methodology for the 21st Century* as a companion book to *Understanding Teaching*. It was edited and parts of it rewritten by my personal friend and former ETA President, Dr. Jonathan Thigpen. Thigpen's contributions to the 2001 edition included topics like the importance of philosophy, research of that day, and how to apply teaching principles to specific age groups, to name only a few.

There has long been a debate as to what constitutes effective teaching. The fact that ETA has been involved in regularly updating their publications is evidence of their commitment to excellence and quality teaching. It's difficult to define what effective teaching looks like without thinking about a person. Maybe the question should be "Who is an effective teacher?" The person—or perhaps people—who comes to your mind as being effective has more than likely demonstrated the *what*. But what made them effective? Why do you still remember them? That's what this book is about. Anyone who has been teaching for any length of time is aware that learning to teach effectively is a constant and ongoing process, and rightly it should be. Culture, technology, and changing knowledge all demand that the process be ongoing.

This book is an attempt to define effective teaching by looking at three aspects. First, the *what* of effective teaching will be observed by studying the life of Jesus Christ as the ultimate educator. In reality, He is by far the greatest *who* of effective teaching. You cannot separate *what* and *how* He taught from the nature of His character. His earthly ministry was basically that of a teacher. As such, He displayed five characteristics: (1) He demonstrated what He said; (2) He desired to serve; (3) He was discerning of His students; (4) He was dedicated to the Scriptures; and (5) He was diverse in His situations. Each of these traits is presented in Section One.

Secondly, this book will once again examine one of the most influential books for Christian Teachers, *The Seven Laws of Teaching*, by John Milton Gregory. His work was first published in 1884 and revised in 1954, but it is still considered one of the greatest publications regarding effective teaching. I will review it in this book for the purpose of comparing those laws of teaching with what some of the most recent research says about teaching. Obviously, in one small volume such as this, we cannot cover every aspect of what research has discovered about effective teaching. That said, this volume will focus on what some educators believe to be the most recent research regarding effective teaching, namely *What Great Teachers Do Differently (14 Things That Matter Most)* by Todd Whitaker. Be advised that the research deals primarily with secular education and educators, but there is much to be gained for those of us in Christian Education. Of interest is to see if the research of today coincides with that of Gregory's laws of years gone by. In addition to presenting the more formal research of Whitaker, I will include additional characteristics of effective teaching from my personal observations and experiences with teachers who have had an impact on my ministry. The seven laws of teaching, what research says about effective teaching, and other characteristics are presented in Section Two.

The third aspect will be more practical in nature. I have learned there are two basic ingredients in any teaching situation: *Preparation and Presentation.* You cannot have one without the other. If one is lacking, the other one comes up short. If both are ready, teaching becomes effective. What are the areas in which effective teachers should be prepared? How do you make an effective presentation? These will be studied in Section Three.

In this book, we'll focus on three aspects of effective teaching, including the use of biblical illustrations, research, and preparation and presentation. Jonathan Thigpen called these elements "...a set of principles which move toward a goal" (Teaching Techniques, p. 7). In essence, these three concepts describe my philosophy of Christian Education. This book is not meant to replace any of the contributions of those who have preceded me. Quite the contrary. It's an attempt to build on the knowledge they have already presented. Look at the subtitle of this book: ... *Becoming An Effective Teacher.* This book is an attempt to show that effective teaching **IS** a continual process. Christian teachers should always be "...becoming..." To be effective demands change. Not change in the basic principles of truth as taught in Scripture, but change in methods, preparation and presentation, and mannerisms.

It is my desire that Christian teachers seek to be like Christ by emulating His five traits as a teacher. My hope is that Christian teachers allow what research says we can, and must, do to improve our ministry. I want to challenge and encourage you as a Christian teacher to be so prepared that when you make your presentation, you make a lasting impression on your students like those who have left their impression on you. One other observation needs to be noted. The original publication of *Teaching Techniques*, and the revisions that followed, described a variety of classroom methods that were appropriate for teachers to use. This edition is not so much about the methods a teacher may use but more about the personality and mannerisms the teacher exibits. In other words, the greatest teaching technique is actually to improve the teacher as a person.

JESUS CHRIST,
THE ULTIMATE EDUCATOR

"There was a man of the Pharisees, named Nicodemus, a ruler of the Jews: The same came to Jesus by night, and said unto him, Rabbi, we know That thou art a teacher come from God: for no man can do these miracles that thou doest, except God be with him."
John 3:1−2

I

You have probably read the above passage many times. It is not important in this presentation to discuss why Nicodemus came by night. The fact is that he came, and that's more than you can say for some people. What is important is what Nicodemus called Jesus. Get the picture? Here are two men educated in the teachings of Jewish law, but there are differences between them. Nicodemus uses four different terms when speaking about Jesus. First, he calls Jesus "Rabbi." The word rabbi means master, or one who is considered highly knowledgeable, particularly in Jewish law, customs, and religion. Secondly, Nicodemus calls Jesus "Teacher" which, once again, is his way of recognizing not only the knowledge of Jesus, but also His position and ability to impart knowledge on others. Thirdly, Nicodemus says of Jesus, "...you are a teacher come from God..." and finally, "...except God be with him." Please note that Nicodemus was aware of the fact that Jesus did not just come from an educational institute where He was trained. He came from God. Nicodemus was trained, but he knew Jesus was much different than him. Jesus Himself even referred to Nicodemus as a teacher as well when He said of him, "...are you a teacher of Israel..." What is literally said is, "Are you Israel's teacher?"

In the earthly ministry of Jesus, He was seldom called a preacher, but often He was referred to as a teacher. Words like taught, teach, and teaching are used frequently about Him. The origin of the following quote has long been forgotten, but the truth of it lingers on:

> "When Jesus was a teacher, it was His passion. He was not teaching when He wasn't doing something else, but when He wasn't doing something else, He was teaching. Teaching was His life."

Even in secular history, there are those who are skeptical about Christ being the Redeemer of the world or even being the Son of God, but many of those skeptics profess that Jesus was a great teacher. But what was it about Him that made His teaching so outstanding? Why were people drawn to Him? How was He so different from other teachers of the day? Why is He still so different today? We could even ask the question, was Jesus really a rabbi? Obviously, He had an advantage over those of us who teach because He was God in the flesh. But when you separate out that part of His life, are there traits or characteristics He possessed that we can emulate? We know very little about His childhood and youth and we don't even know for sure that as an adult that He was trained as a rabbi. Yet those who heard Him teach were often astonished. What we do know is that He was prepared.

His Preparation to Become a Teacher

His preparation may be seen in three different periods of life that were silent. In other words, there are three eras in His life that we know very little about, but there is significance in that silence. The first period of silence is from the day of His birth until He was only eight days old. All we know for sure is that when He was eight days old He experienced the Jewish custom of being circumcised (Luke 2:21–35). It may seem unimportant, but read the passage carefully and you'll see that Simon, who was the one overseeing this event, recognized this baby was not just an ordinary baby. He was the *"salvation"* that had been promised. What happened during that first week of His infancy is not known. But don't disregard it.

The second period of silence is from the time He was eight days old until He was twelve years of age. We know then that He was taken to the temple in Jerusalem. In Jewish custom, even today, this is known as a Jewish boy's Bar Mitzvah, or the time he is considered to have reached an age of religious and civic responsibility. You may recall that those who were listening to Him could not believe what they were hearing. In fact, Luke says, "...all that heard him were astonished at his understanding and answers" (Luke 2:47). Luke further reports that Jesus went home with Mary and Joseph and fulfilled His obligation to be an obedient son. There are those in secular history who speculate that during this time Jesus may have performed several miracles, such as turning clay pigeons into live ones, to display His power and show off for Mary and Joseph. However, when you read the account of His earthly ministry and the beginning of His miracles, John the writer makes it very plain that when Jesus turned the water into wine, His first miracle, this was the "...beginning of miracles..." (John 2:11).

The third period of silence was when Jesus was twelve years of age to about the age of thirty. Our society puts great emphasis on this time in the lives of modern children and even calls it a rite of passage and the age of adolescence, but not so with Jesus. Why was it a period of silence? As with the other two periods of silence, this era was a time of being trained by Jewish parents but more important, it was a time of fulfilling all the requirements of the Jewish law. Children were to obey their parents. Jesus did that. The oldest son in the family was to take care of his mother in the event of her husband's death. Jesus did that as well. The oldest son was to be sure his mother would be taken care of, should something happen to him. Jesus did that by telling John the Apostle to take Mary as his own mother (John 19:25–27) when Jesus was about to be crucified. Tradition, and even parts of the Law, stated that an individual could not enter a ministry, such as serving as a rabbi, until he was at least thirty years of age, and Jesus did that. In other words, Jesus was recognized as a reliable Jewish teacher because His very life had exemplified obedience to the teachings of the Jewish people. In His earthly ministry, had He not fulfilled the obligations as spelled out in the Law, He would have lost His credibility. Because of His life, His credibility was recognized.

He Demonstrated What He Said

You're familiar with the old adage, "I'd rather see a sermon than hear one." You are aware of the opposite one that says, "Don't do as I do; do as I say." The first one is effective. The second one is ineffective. Whatever the topic when Jesus was speaking, He was His own illustration. He not only illustrated his point, He personified it. That may be one of the reasons His critics could find nothing wrong with Him. The truths He taught were seen in His life, or as we say, He practiced what He preached. To illustrate this trait, note a few of the topics He taught on and then search for others on your own.

Prayer: *"Then cometh Jesus with them unto a place called Gethsemane, and saith unto the disciples, Sit ye here, while I go and pray yonder"* (Matthew 26:36).

Obedience: *"And he went a little farther, and fell on his face, and prayed, saying, O my Father, if it be possible, let this cup pass from me: nevertheless, not as I will, but as thou wilt"* (Matthew 26:39).

Submission to authority: *"Notwithstanding, lest we should offend them, go thou to the sea, and cast an hook, and take up the fish that first cometh up;*

and when thou hast opened his mouth, thou shalt find a piece of money: that take, and give unto them for me and thee" (Matthew 17:27).

Concern for parents: *"When Jesus therefore saw his mother, and the disciple standing by, whom he loved, he saith unto his mother, Woman, behold they son! Then saith he to the disciple, Behold thy mother! And from that hour that disciple took her unto his own home"* (John 19:26–27; Read also Luke 2:51).

Humility/servanthood: *"If I then, your Lord and Master, have washed your feet; ye also ought to wash one another's feet"* (John 13:14).

Forgiveness: *"Then said Jesus, Father forgive them; for they know not what they do. And they parted his raiment, and cast lots"* (Luke 23:34).

Love: *"This is my commandment, That ye love one another, as I have loved you"* (John 15:12).

One of the problems we often have in church settings is that some people talk one way but live another. Not so with Jesus. Even parents at times are guilty of saying one thing but doing another. Not Jesus. If you are a teacher, I can assure you that students watch you when you don't know they're watching. It behooves us to be examples of our faith in the presence of others. Jesus taught that we should be like Him. James says, "But be ye doers of the word and not hearers only..." (James 1:22). James further adds that to not be a doer deceives others, and it actually deceives you. Note even further that James not only tells us to be an example, or demonstrate our words, but to demonstrate our work as well. He puts it like this: "...But a doer of the work, this man shall be blessed in his deed" (James 1:25). Jesus certainly demonstrated what James states. Look carefully at the life of the Lord as a teacher and you cannot help but notice He demonstrated what He taught in front of those who heard Him. We should do no less.

In Section Two, *What Research Tells Us about Effective Teaching*, you will see what Todd Whitaker and his team discovered about effective teaching. However, in light of Jesus demonstrating what He said, you need to read some of the key concepts Whitaker explains that are related to this point. Read the following very carefully:

"We can always learn from observing what great teachers do. Eliminating inappropriate choices does not help as much as identifying good ideas used by successful educators."

"All that is truly needed to improve education is for all teachers to be like our very best teachers."

"What matters most is not what teachers do...but how appropriately and effectively they do it."

For Further Discussion

1. Summarize in your own words the conversation between Jesus and Nicodemus as recorded in John 3:1–10.

2. Jesus is often referred to as a teacher, but seldom as a preacher. What is the difference between the two?

3. How do you think the three silent periods in the life of Jesus prepared Him for His earthly ministry? Do you think the silence is significant? Why or why not?

4. What are some other areas in which Jesus demonstrated what He said in addition to those listed?

5. How important is it for teachers to be an example of what they teach? Explain how not being a good example can have a negative influence.

6. To what do you attribute the success of the teaching ministry of Jesus?

7. Think back in your days of education and remember a teacher who left a good impression on you. What made that impression?

8. Think back in your days of education and remember a teacher who left a bad impression on you. What made that impression?

Notes

1. *Study Guide: What Great Teachers Do Differently (14 Things That Matter Most)*, p. 1

HE DESIRED TO SERVE
He Was Discerning of His Students

2

You may recall the story of an overzealous mother in the Bible, Salome, the wife of Zebedee, and the mother of James and John. It's recorded in Matthew 20:20–28 and Mark 10:35–45. She wanted Jesus to allow her two sons to sit with Him in lofty positions when Jesus was to set up His kingdom. The entire conversation made the other ten disciples quite upset to the point they were "...moved with indignation..." (Matthew 20:24). You can decide for yourself if the ten disciples were mad at James and John and their mother, or aggravated with themselves for not asking Jesus the same question, or maybe it was a little bit of both. Either way, Jesus used this occasion to teach His disciples a valuable lesson regarding service to others. Notice what Jesus said: "...whosoever will be great among you, let him be your minister; and whosoever will be chief among you, let him be your servant" (Matthew 20:26, 27). To further prove His point, Jesus said, "Even as the Son of man came not to be ministered unto, but to minister..." (Matthew 20:28). The obvious point is that Jesus lived His earthly life in service to others. In essence, what He said was this: "I didn't come for you to serve me. I came to serve you."

The question then becomes, did Jesus serve others, and if so, when and how? Perhaps an even greater question is, why did Jesus serve others? After all, He certainly deserved to be served Himself. It goes against the very nature of what we are taught, for a greater person to serve a lesser person. We are taught that those in positions of leadership and authority are more important and we treat them as such. Look how we treat a boss at work, a supervisor on the job, a celebrity, or even elected officials. Look how we treat the President of the United States. We don't expect them to serve us; we serve them. Yet Jesus is far greater than any boss, supervisor, celebrity, elected official, or president, and He says He came to serve us. You might be thinking, that's all well and good, but Jesus didn't encounter the kind of people we deal with. We've got that backwards. We haven't encountered the kind of people Jesus did, or maybe we have. The point is, humanity is basically the same. Generations may come and go, but personalities and temperaments have a way of being similar throughout time. He was a servant to all kinds of people, sometimes to the point that He confronted those we have a tendency to shun or avoid completely. Space constraints do not allow for a complete listing of the kinds of people Jesus encountered, but a few examples will certainly verify He desired to serve. As you look at the following examples, note as well a third trait Jesus possessed: He was discerning of His students. His desire to serve and His discernment of those He served are so related that you need to see them as actually being one. One other important factor we need to realize is this: Jesus possessed an intuitive knowledge of His students that we don't have. That gave Him an obvious advantage, but the simple truth remains that effective teachers know something about the students they teach.

Nicodemus

Read the account again in John 3:1–10. As you read that familiar story, notice the kind of person Nicodemus was. He was a ruler; he was more than likely a rabbi; he was considered highly educated; he was religious. Tradition says he was more than likely a member of the Sanhedrin, a religious council of men who were known to either be a chief priest, a scribe, or an elder. They represented the aristocrats of the day in both politics and religion. Jesus knew all of that, so His conversation with Nicodemus was more theological than practical. Jesus knew that Nicodemus had some serious questions about Jewish laws and salvation, but Jesus did not shy away from those questions. He welcomed them. He challenged Nicodemus to think. Jesus did not put Nicodemus down because of his doubts and questions. Quite frankly, Nicodemus was the type that many of us would rather not talk to. He would probably intimidate us, but not so with Jesus. If this story shows anything at all, it certainly proves that everyone is in need of salvation, even those we might call "upper crust." Jesus had a desire to serve the likes of Nicodemus.

Woman at the Well

Her story is recorded in John 4:7–29. There is an obvious contrast between this woman and Nicodemus. Whatever Nicodemus was, she was the opposite. Whatever you think of a woman of ill-repute, she was probably that and a whole lot more; yet Jesus desired to be of service to her, just as much as he desired to serve those of the upper class.

You may recall a similar story in John 8:1–11. This account shows two different women to be sure, but both needed what Jesus could offer. In both cases, Jesus knew the people involved very well. His desire to serve these women is clearly seen in how He reacted to them. They represented one of the worst kinds of sinners, yet Jesus dealt with them with compassion and even dignity. It's amazing how accepting Jesus was with the worst of sinners, and how harsh He often was with religious hypocrites. Our culture too often gets that backwards. Don't forget that Jesus Himself said He came not to help those who were well but those who needed help (Mark 2:17).

The Apostle Peter

Do you know anyone like the Apostle Peter? It could be one of your students. Peter liked to brag about what he could do, but too often that's all it was: bragging. On one occasion Peter bragged that he was willing to die for Christ, but then later he was afraid to tell the truth about his affiliation with Him. You've seen that kind. Peter was one of those who suffered from "foot and mouth disease." He was the type who forgot to put his brain in gear before he opened his mouth. He also represents people who, when they finally get thoroughly right with God, become powerful in their work for God. Once that happens, you'd better watch out. They're going to do great things for God. Jesus was willing to be of service to Peter and to be patient with him because He knew his future potential. What would have happened if Jesus had not been willing to serve Peter? We'll never know that answer, but what we do know is that a loud, foul-mouthed, arrogant fisherman became one of the greatest tools on the day of Pentecost (Acts 2:14–36) and the author of two books in the New Testament. Jesus' attitude towards Peter should teach us not to give up on those who have his personality and temperament.

A Widow

Are you seeing a pattern develop in these people Jesus was willing to serve? He served the religious, the scholarly Nicodemus, the unrighteous, the woman at the well, and the arrogant such as the Apostle Peter. One of the classes of people often overlooked are the widows. What do they have to offer? Why should we be concerned about them? Jesus provides the answers. Her story is told in Luke 21:1–4. We don't know very much about her, but Jesus knew something about her that others had never thought about. You know the story. People were making their way to place an offering in the treasury of the temple. The rich were making their offering, which was money taken from their abundance. The widow put in "...two mites..." which was the equivalent of less than five cents. In her day, a mite was the smallest coin made. Even the metal from which it was made was considered inferior. It was smaller in size than our penny. More than likely, the rich donors fascinated those standing around, watching people put money in a receptacle. It seems the only one who saw this widow was Jesus, but He used her as an illustration that showed it's not the amount of money a person gives but the attitude of the heart. The rich gave of their abundance.

She literally gave all she had. In fact, the King James Version says she gave of her "...penury..." or out of her poverty. Her contribution, however, has brought her notoriety. We get our expression "the widow's mite" from her story. Don't miss the point. Jesus knew her. Jesus knew the rich people too, but He didn't praise them. He praised her. Let this be a vivid reminder for us to never overlook any student, even those who, like the widow, seem insignificant to worldly eyes.

Thomas

The life of Thomas and his attitude of doubt should be an encouragement to all of us. For one thing, we need to be reminded that it's not always wrong to doubt. Doubt can sometimes be helpful, particularly when it drives us to resolve the doubt. Thomas' account is found in John 20:24–29. Again, note how kindly Jesus handled Thomas. To be sure, Thomas felt the reprimand of the Lord, but it was said in such a way that Thomas was not offended by it. You must understand that doubt is not the same as unbelief. Dr. Cheryl L. Fawcett, in ETA's *Understanding People*, says it like this: "...(doubt) is a faith that has not made up its mind yet..." (p. 55). Jesus did not turn away those who doubted. He desired to help them. On another occasion when Jesus encountered an individual who doubted, that person said what many of us have thought as well: "...Lord, I believe; help thou mine unbelief" (Mark 9:24). To not be willing to serve those who have doubts is to drive them away. Be like Jesus and be willing to serve even the doubters.

Nathaniel

Not much is known about Nathaniel. You can read about him in John 1:45–51. For our discussion, I'll simply include these words about him from Jesus: "... Before that Philip called thee, when thou wast under the fig tree, I saw thee." It's not the purpose here to discuss what Nathaniel was doing under the fig tree. Our purpose is to point out once again that Jesus knew something about him. Jesus even called him "...an Israelite indeed, in whom is no guile." Jesus not only knew his geographical location—He knew Nathaniel's character.

Look at the list of people Jesus desired to serve. They include some of the most sinful, repulsive, and stubborn people. We still have those kinds of people today in our churches and classes. They come in a variety of ages and genders. They come from different backgrounds and cultures. They come from different socioeconomic and educational backgrounds, but they all have one thing in common: they need us. Like Jesus, we should seek to minister to them. We should not push them aside. One of the key concepts from Todd Whitaker's research is stated like this: "Effective teachers focus on the future and what they (students, people) have the ability to influence, not on what has already happened." (*Study Guide, What Great Teachers Do Differently: 14 Things That Matter Most*, p. 13). In other words, like Jesus, we must look beyond what students are and see what they can become. That can only happen when we desire to serve them.

Teachers who teach five days a week know the importance of knowing students. In Christian education, your teaching may be limited to only one or two times per week, but the need is still the same. You need to know something about them. What is their name? Where do they live? To whom are they related? What are their interests? When you know something about them, you're better prepared to meet their needs. When you glean insight into who they are as people outside of the classroom, you have a different attitude about them. Care must be exercised to not become too snoopy, but expressing a genuine interest in them will pay great dividends. In the research completed by Todd Whitaker, one of his key concepts is this: "Our own perception of our school and our students impacts the reality of our school and students. Teachers have the power to decide the tone of their school and how teachers in their school view their students" (*Study Guide, What Great Teachers Do Differently, 14 Things That Matter Most*, p. 33). In other words, your attitude about your church, the class you teach, and the students is directly related to how much they learn or don't learn.

For Further Discussion

1. Think of other individuals Jesus served besides those listed in this chapter.

2. While it's important to know something about students, discuss the importance of keeping confidences when a student confides in you.

3. Look at the individuals presented in this chapter and discuss what kind of personality and/or temperament you think they might have had.

4. Discuss how society in general often ignores certain kinds of people while praising others. What makes the difference in how we treat them?

5. In your opinion, how do you think the people presented in this chapter responded to the way Jesus was willing to serve them?

6. What are some of the areas of Christianity that give you possible doubt?

HE WAS DEDICATED TO THE SCRIPTURES

3

Since you are reading this, you are probably involved in teaching others, or you at least have an interest in it. You're to be commended for that. Hopefully, you have an interest in obtaining knowledge of the Bible. Again, you're to be commended. One of the greatest tragedies of many people in church today is their lack of Biblical knowledge. As a teacher who strives to emulate the teaching traits of Jesus Christ, it is imperative that you be committed to the authority of the Scriptures. Just a casual reading of the New Testament reveals that Jesus was dedicated to the Scriptures. Again, He had an advantage over us. He helped in the writing of them. But as you read, begin to notice how often in the ministry of our Lord He made references to the Scriptures. When He was challenged by those who claimed to believe the Scriptures, He would say something like, "What did Moses say?" or "Have you never read?"

Reread the story of Jesus being tempted by the devil in the wilderness in Matthew 4:4, 7, 10 and notice the reaction of Jesus.

> *Matthew 4:4: "Be he answered and said, <u>It is written</u>, Man shall not live by bread alone but by every word that proceedeth out of the mouth of God."*

> *Matthew 4:7: "Jesus said unto him, <u>It is written</u> again, Thou shalt not tempt the Lord thy God."*

> *Matthew 4:10: "Then saith Jesus unto him, Get thee hence, Satan: for <u>it is written</u>, Thou shalt worship the Lord Thy God, and him only shalt thou serve."*

Three times Jesus was tempted and three times He said, "...it is written..." He knew the Scriptures well. If in His body of flesh He had to resort to the Scriptures, how much more do we? It has been said that the Bible is the best commentary on itself. That is easily illustrated in this story. In 1 John 2:16, we are told that every temptation we receive comes from one of three sources. Another passage in Hebrews 4:15 states this same truth. Notice these two passages:

1 John 2:16: "For all that is in the world, the lust of the flesh, and the lust of the eyes, and the pride of life, is not of the Father, but is of the world."

Hebrews 4:15: "For we have not an high priest which cannot be touched with the feeling of our infirmities; but was in all points tempted like as we are, yet without sin."

Interestingly enough, that was true with Jesus as well. Take those same three areas and apply them to the temptation of Jesus:

Temptation (Matthew 4:3, 6, 8)	Area (I John 2:16)
Make the stones bread, v. 3	*lust of the flesh, 1 John 2:16*
Cast thyself down, v. 6	*pride of life*
All the kingdoms of the world, v. 8	*lust of the eyes*

You must understand that these three temptations were real. They were not artificial. Prior to this, the Lord was led into the wilderness where He stayed and fasted for forty days. It was after He had not eaten for forty days that Satan tempted Him to make bread out of the stones. Satan knew Jesus had the ability to do that and Satan knew Jesus was hungry. Many of us have a hard time staying on a diet, much less not eating for several days. Jesus could have made bread out of the stones but to do so would be submitting to the devil. In the physical flesh, Jesus was hungry, but in His divinity, Jesus was dedicated to the Scriptures.

The devil also knew that should Jesus have jumped off the pinnacle of the temple, a host of angels could have come to His rescue. It would have been a spectacular sight to see a host of angels swooping down from heaven to rescue Jesus. In His humanity, that was a temptation related to the pride of life and to surrender to that would once again be submitting to the devil.

This world is a beautiful place. Think of some of the most beautiful places you have seen. Picture the eight wonders of the world, or the beautiful manifestations of creation like a rainbow, a sunrise, a sunset, and the changing of the seasons. Think of the magnificent buildings of government like the White House in Washington, D.C., the House of Parliament in England, or the Louvre in Paris. It was these kinds of things that the devil was tempting Jesus with. The eye-gate is one of the devil's greatest allurements to our flesh. Yet Jesus refused to submit to the temptation of the lust of the eyes. He overcame all three of these temptations because He was dedicated to the Scriptures.

What does it mean to be dedicated to the Scriptures? Is it really that important? Every believer should be a student of the Word of God. There's no excuse for Christian teachers to be ignorant of the Bible. You may not have had the privilege of attending a Christian school or a Bible college, but that does not excuse you for not knowing the Bible. The Apostle Peter makes that very plain when he says, "...and be ready always to give an answer to every man that asketh you a reason of the hope that is in you..." (1 Peter 3:15). When you trace the ministry of Christ, whenever He was faced with unbelievers, scoffers, or skeptics, He was always ready to give an answer. If we are to be followers of Christ, particularly as Christian teachers, we can do no less. Obviously, to be ready to give an answer means we need to know why we believe the Bible. However, our answers should not be given in a spirit of arrogance or superiority. Peter spoke to that as well when he said, "...with meekness and fear..." (1 Peter 3:15).

In this day of technology, there are literally hundreds of resources available to anyone who has a desire to know more about the Bible. Things like Christian radio and television that promote good, Bible-filled content abound. The Internet itself makes it possible to receive instant information. By going to "Google" and merely typing in any question, you have immediate access to more information than you can possibly read. Good Bible-believing teachers have many resources available for use in the privacy of your home or office. You can play a CD while you drive. Yes, you have to be selective, and yes, you have to use discernment, but doing nothing should not be an option for the Christian teacher who wants to be like Christ.

Being dedicated to the Scriptures has some obvious characteristics. Here are a few:

1. Having a regular, consistent time to read the Bible yourself

2. Letting the Bible be the final authority when you are faced with tough issues

3. Having a working knowledge of the Bible that includes:

    a. Knowing some of the history of the origin of the Bible

    b. Knowing something about each of the books of the Bible, like who the author is, to whom the author is speaking, and what the subject matter is

    c. Knowing something about the culture of the time and events that occur in the Bible

4. Not being afraid, or embarrassed, to question things you don't understand

5. Keeping reading and studying until you find your answers

6. Having discussions with other believers

7. Having a desire to learn and understand and a teachable spirit

8. Knowing some of the basic terms that are related to the understanding of the Bible, such as:

   a. *Inspiration*: God's breath upon the writers of the Bible to assure accuracy and truth (Read 2 Timothy 3:16 and 2 Peter 1:20, 21)

   b. *Revelation*: God giving information to the writers of the Bible that they could not have known any other way

   c. *Application*: Making the truths of the Bible personal and relevant in the life of a believer

   d. *Inerrant*: The Bible in its original form was without error or mistake. Plenary verbal refers to the fact that each and every word was the exact word God intended.

   e. *Infallible:* without fault; completely accurate and true

   f. *Doctrine:* a systematic way of understanding a given topic of the Bible, such as the doctrine of Scriptures, doctrine of God, doctrine of Jesus Christ, etc.

9. Teaching from Scripture itself instead of a teacher's manual as you make your presentation

10. Being able to tell in your own words why you believe the Bible is true

It is to be acknowledged that there are differing views regarding which translation should be used in reading and studying the Bible. Granted, spiritual discernment must be used when deciding which translation is ultimately selected. Remember to demonstrate appreciation and respect for others who have differing views. Years ago this author had the privilege of hearing the late Theodore Epp of the popular radio broadcast, *Back To The Bible*. For five days, his topic dealt with different versions of the Bible. Every day he would explain why it was necessary, and beneficial, to have different translations. He would close each program with this: "On Friday, I'm going to tell you the best translation of the Bible you should read." I listened faithfully. I respected his judgment and wanted to know which translation this godly man was going to recommend. Friday came and I was certain to be tuned in. Once again, he dealt with the topic and then he said, "Now I'm going to tell you the best translation of the Bible to read. Are you ready?" I was in my car but I caught myself answering back, "Yes." Then he said, "The best translation of the Bible you should read is the one you will read." I couldn't believe what I was hearing. I thought, "Is that all there is?" But as I have contemplated that statement, he was right. Reading a different translation is better than not reading any translation. The one you will read is the one you will come to understand. Not reading any translation is to ignore the example of Christ by not being dedicated to the Scriptures.

For Further Discussion

1. Discuss further with your class the fact that all temptations come from one of three different sources as mentioned in 1 John 2:16 and Hebrews 4:15.

2. Discuss the temptation of Jesus. How was His temptation similar to the temptations all people face?

3. Name some ways you can tell people why you believe what you believe about the Bible.

4. Discuss some practical ways to gain personal knowledge about the Bible.

5. Discuss some ways to determine the validity of a Bible translation.

6. Discuss some of the things Bible writers could not have known had God not given them direct information.

7. Discuss this statement: *The Bible is both complete and completed.* (Are there individuals today who have inspiration on their lives in the same way Bible writers did? Are there individuals today who have the ability to receive "new" revelations concerning the future?)

HE WAS DIVERSE IN HIS SITUATIONS

4

If you have been teaching for any length of time, you should be keenly aware of the fact that diversity in the classroom is a necessity. Diversity brings vitality to both the spirit of the classroom and the individual students. It also creates a renewed energy in the teacher. You cannot study the teaching style of Jesus without recognizing that He used diversity. His diversity is seen in three distinct areas: His classroom, His content, and His conduct.

His Classroom

In chapter one of this book there is a statement that says, "When Jesus was a teacher, it was His passion. He was not teaching when He wasn't doing something else, but when He wasn't doing something else, He was teaching. Teaching was His life." We'll see in this section how He evidenced this truth throughout His ministry. Wherever He was, He was teaching. His classroom was anywhere and everywhere. He didn't need a particular place or room. The four Gospels—Matthew, Mark, Luke, and John—describe some of the places where He taught, but a quick survey through the Gospel of John illustrates the variety of classrooms in which Jesus taught:

- At night (John 3:2)
- On the side of a well (John 4:6–13)
- On the side of a mountain (John 6:3)
- In a boat (John 6:22)
- In the temple (John 7:14; 8:2)
- In the open air/daytime (John 9:1–7)
- In a private home (John 11:20)
- In a graveyard (John 11:38–44)
- In an upper room (John 13:1–20; 14:1–31)
- In a garden (John 15; 18:1–27)
- Before Pilate (John 18:28–40)
- In a closed room (John 20:19)

Jesus was well aware that teaching is not confined to a certain hour of the day, a particular day of the week, or a specific location. Teaching is wherever and whenever a willing teacher happens to be with one or more people who want to learn. It is very possible that your own effectiveness as a teacher would be enhanced by varying your location. I personally remember a time when I was teaching the Gospel of John at a Bible college and I took students to a local cemetery that had a replica of the tomb of Jesus. The class went there when we studied the Resurrection. Being in the replica of that tomb made the truth of the Resurrection more realistic. Look around your community. Look around your own church. Find a different location to use on occasion. Visit a classroom and see how other teachers use variety. Good teachers are constantly looking for something and someplace different. If you can't go to another location, rearrange the one you have.

His Content

His content in many ways depended upon His audience. It often depended on what He already knew about His students. He knew how simple to be or how much He could challenge their intellect. Again, He possessed intuitive knowledge where you and I have to work at knowing our students, but every effective teacher knows how important it is to combine learning and knowledge with the specific needs of the students. Sometimes Jesus became engaged in deep theological discussions like He did with Nicodemus and the scribes and Pharisees. Other times He taught spiritual truth by being very plain and simple. His content and method were often one and the same. Here are just a few samples of how simple His content was:

- The wind (John 3:8; Matthew 8:23–27)
- Birds (Matthew 6:26)
- Flowers (Matthew 6:28)
- Seed (Matthew 13:1–23)
- Mustard seed (Matthew 13:31, 32)
- Treasure and costly pearls (Matthew 13:44–46)
- Salt (Matthew 5:13)
- Light (Matthew 5:14)
- Bread (John 6:35; 48, 51)

Look at that list again. To this very day we have experiences with almost every one of the items mentioned. In other words, some of the greatest spiritual truths are seen in the simple everyday experiences of life. Every effective teacher knows the power of a good illustration. An illustration can make hard things simple. Jesus knew that and utilized it in His teaching. There's a time and place to be very deep and intelligent, but the fact remains that most people today need truths that are easy to grasp. One educator of many years ago illustrated it like this: A mouse and a giraffe were seen eating out in the same field. The mouse could not reach up to the high limbs like the giraffe, but the giraffe could bend down to eat the grass. Apply that to your teaching. All students need to have lessons taught at their own level if they are to really grasp the truths presented.

There's another adage that students are known to say about teachers: some teachers make hard things simple while other teachers make simple things hard. Which one are you? Unfortunately, some teachers seek to impress students with their knowledge and while they may succeed in making an impression, it will not be effective.

His Conduct

"His conduct" refers to the methods and procedures Jesus used when dealing with people. We have noted the classrooms or *where* He taught, the content, or *what* He taught, and now we will examine His conduct, or *how* He taught. The point is, every experienced teacher is keenly aware that these three (what, where, and how) are important to effective teaching. Todd Whitaker verifies this fact in his research. Whitaker and his team of researchers state this: "Who we are as teachers and what we do as teachers is more important that what we know. Teachers must self-reflect on who they are and what they must do in order to improve their practice. What matters most is not what teachers do…but how appropriately and effectively they do it" *(Study Guide, What Great Teachers Do Differently: 14 Things That Matter Most,* p. 1).

Every teacher is interested in using the most appropriate methods available. Obviously, the methods available today were not available in the days of Jesus, but when you look closely at what He did, you get the idea that He was concerned about His methods. Here is just a brief sample of some of His methods:

• Visuals

• One-on-one

• Small groups

- Large groups

- Discussions

- Questions and answers

- Hypothetical situations

- Thought-provoking illustrations

These methods are still in use today. Years ago I was introduced to a Christian company known as Faith Visuals. It was a company that specialized in the training of Christian teachers, particularly in the use of visual aids. PowerPoint had not yet come on the scene, but this company knew how to effectively use an overhead projector, even giving it motion. In one of the presentations, the leader said this: "If Jesus were alive today, He would use an overhead projector." Today, she would probably add, "If Jesus were alive today, He'd use PowerPoint." Her point was that Jesus was proficient in using what was available and He knew the importance of making a visual impression on the minds of His students. That may have been a tongue-in-cheek comment, but her point should be well-taken.

There is one important point, however, regarding the use of methods and visual aids that needs to be stressed. You as a teacher ARE an audio-visual. You have a voice that can be lowered or made louder. You have a body that can be animated and used as a means of demonstrating a point. You have the ability to smile or frown, to cry or laugh. You may not feel comfortable using equipment such as PowerPoint and other visuals, but make use of the audio-visual you already have: yourself.

For Further Discussion

1. Review the variety of places where Jesus taught. Which one seems to appeal to you the most? Which one does not appeal to you?

2. Ask your students to suggest some ways to add diversity to their class time.

3. Discuss some things it would be good to know about your students. (Be sure to stress that keeping confidences is vital.)

THE SEVEN LAWS OF TEACHING

5

You've heard the expression, "history repeats itself." That is certainly true when it comes to the truths outlined in *The Seven Laws of Teaching*. John Milton Gregory wrote this well-known book on the discipline of education. It was first published in 1884, revised in 1954, and still continues to be used as a resource for effective teaching today. Former President of ETA Jonathan Thigpen, in writing about this in an earlier edition of *Teaching Techniques*, said this: "Although much important educational research has been done in the past century, it has only supported Gregory's basis positions, confirming why they are true" (*Teaching Techniques*, 2003 Edition, p. 15).

This chapter seeks to accomplish three things. First, it will explain each of the seven laws as outlined by Milton Gregory. Secondly, it will list some of the comments presented in the 2003 edition of *Teaching Techniques* by Jonathan Thigpen. Thirdly, Gregory's original thoughts will be compared, as appropriate and available, with the research of Todd Whitaker presented in *What Great Teachers Do Differently: 14 Things That Matter Most*. As you read the seven laws and compare them to the research, take note of the things you may need to do to continue to improve your personal effectiveness as a teacher.

Law #1: The Law of the Teacher: *The teacher must know that which is to be taught.*

This law refers to the importance of the teacher having an in-depth knowledge of the subject matter at hand. That is true regardless of the subject. this practice is of extreme importance to those of us who teach the Bible and other related subjects. With this in mind, Jonathan Thigpen commented: "As a Christian teacher, you must have knowledge in several key areas:[1]

1. You must know without a doubt that you have a personal, vital, and growing relationship with God through His Son, Jesus Christ.

2. You must be a diligent student of the Word of God.

3. You should possess the spiritual gift of teaching (Romans 12:3–8).

4. You should be convinced of God's power to change the life of anyone who turns to Him in faith.

5. You should seek to know everything possible about the students you teach.

6. You should constantly strive to learn everything possible about becoming a better teacher. Never forget that you are a learner too.

Whitaker's research, as it relates to the position of the teacher, states the following:[2]

1. All that is truly needed to improve education is for *all* teachers to be like their very best teachers.

2. *Who we are* as teachers and *what we do* is more important than what we know. Teachers must self-reflect on who they are and what they must do in order to improve their practice.

3. There are really only two ways to improve any school: recruit better teachers or improve the teachers already there. (You may easily substitute the word "church" for "school.")

4. What matters most is not what teachers do, but how appropriately and effectively they do it.

Law #2: The Law of the Learner: *The learner must desire to learn that which is to be taught.*

For years there has been a debate that says if there has been no learning, there has been no teaching. Put another way, if students haven't learned anything, the teacher hasn't taught anything. In recent years, that has been revised to the point that many educators today recognize that the education process is a two-way street. It involves both the teacher and the student. The teacher certainly has a leadership role, but the student must take responsibility for learning as well. The teacher needs to set the stage, or have an environment conducive to learning. Again, Jonathan Thigpen states a teacher must do two things: arrest the attention of the student, and develop it into an interest for the subject.[3]

Whitaker's research reveals the following:[4]

1. Great teachers create a positive atmosphere...despite inevitable negatives...such as limited resources.

2. Great teachers do not "teach to the middle." Instead, they ensure that every student is engaged.

Teachers are keenly aware that the interest of students varies from student to student. Some come with more knowledge than others. Some have little or no knowledge on the subject matter at all. That is an issue that is too often overlooked in a church setting. Just because someone is faithful to Sunday School and church does not mean they have knowledge of some of the most basic spiritual truths. The Bible itself makes that plain in Hebrews 5:11–14. The author of Hebrews describes many of those as:. "...dull of hearing...", "...need of milk...", "...not of strong meat...", "...a babe...". Unfortunately, we may have some of these in our churches and classes. More about this will be said as it relates to the preparation and presentation of the teacher, but for now, just remember that you need to make the class as interesting as you possibly can.

One concept of effective teachers in Christian education that is too often overlooked, or even ignored, is having certain expectations for the student. For too long we have been afraid to have expectations for fear we will drive students away. Besides, this is Sunday School, not regular school, argue some people. But the fact that it is Sunday School, and we are teaching the Bible, is the very reason it should be at least on the same level as public and/or private schools, if not more. In reality, however, it's usually the very opposite. We don't expect much, therefore students think they won't receive much and consequently, it ends up both the teacher and the student may be right. Regarding this, Whitaker's research found the following:[5]

1. Great teachers focus on expectations.

2. Great teachers establish clear expectations—and follow them firmly, fairly, and consistently.

3. Teachers may have varying expectations, but all great teachers set expectations that are clearly established, focused on the future, and consistently reinforced.

It may take some time and effort to establish expectations, but the outcome will be worth it. You may have to start small, but start. Start by expecting students to answer a question that has been asked. When you ask a question, wait until someone answers. Typically, teachers ask a question and when no one responds, and the silence becomes "deafening," the teacher goes ahead and answers the questions. The students know that, so they don't respond. When they learn you mean for someone to respond and you wait in silence, someone will eventually answer. Let them know that you can wait them out. Also, don't just ask a question that can be answered with a "yes" or "no." Ask a question that needs a few more words. They'll get the point.

Law #3: The Law of Language: *The language must be common to both teacher and learner.*

Our English language is an interesting thing. The same word can have different meanings to different people, such as the word "cool." It can refer to the weather or it can refer to something that is really nice or great or even "groovy." A word can be spelled one way but pronounced two different ways, such as the word read. You can say something like, "I read the paper this morning," or you can say, "I'm going to read a good book today." A word can even be spelled two different ways but then pronounced only one way, such as "red" like the car is red, or "read" as in you read the last chapter of this book. Ironically, to a younger generation, two words can be spelled the same way, be pronounced the same way, and still have completely opposite meanings, such as the word "bad." An older generation would define "bad" as something evil or the opposite of good. A younger generation may define it as something that is actually good. Each of these illustrations, and a whole lot more, verify that considering language is vital in the process of communicating when teaching. Effective teachers know that and seek to use the same language as their students. Missionaries know the importance of learning a foreign language in order to communicate the Gospel in an effective way.

Jonathan Thigpen offers the following suggestions regarding the importance of teachers and students being on the same language level:[6]

1. Study the language of the students constantly and carefully.

2. Discern your students' knowledge of the subject.

3. Express yourself in the language of your students.

4. Use simple and few words to express your meaning.

5. To clarify meaning, repeat your thoughts using different words, if possible, and with greater simplicity.

6. Use illustrations to aid in defining words.

7. Try to increase the size of the students' vocabularies, and at the same time clarify the meaning of various words used.

8. Encourage students to talk freely and listen carefully.

To illustrate the importance of good communication, and being on the same language level, look at the following multiple choice test and decide which one sport does not belong in the listing. Be able to explain your reason as well.

    a. Baseball

    b. Hockey

    c. Billiards

    d. Football

If you have been teaching for any length of time, you are aware that testing the knowledge of your students can be difficult because they look at questions you ask with a different attitude than yours. You have one set of answers in your mind and they have another. In the above test, the teacher who actually used this said the correct answer was football. The logic for the answer is that football is the only sport in the group that does not use a stick of some kind. All the others use either a bat, a cue stick, or a hockey stick. The logic is right, but it does not take into account there are other answers that are just as right, such as:

1.   Hockey could be the right answer because all the other sports use a ball; hockey uses a puck. It could also be right because all the other sports have the letter "l" in their name.

2.   Billiards could be the right answer because all the other sports are a team game; billiards can be played alone. It could also be right because billiards is not considered a contact sport while the others are, nor does it have a particular uniform, and it is typically played indoors while the others are usually played outdoors.

3.   Football could also be the right answer because the other sports use a round object while a football is an oval object.

It's possible there are other answers, but don't miss the point. Your answer depends on your definition and knowledge of sports. It's possible that you may not know one of the above sports at all. Teachers often use words they assume students know without realizing the students may have a completely different connotation of the word. It's possible to even use words regarding biblical truth that you assume are common, but the students do not know them at all.

On one occasion I had the privilege of speaking and teaching at a summer youth camp. The camp offered swimming as one of its activities but a lifeguard, who was not a camper or on staff, had to be hired for security reasons. I went swimming one day and wanted to witness to the lifeguard so I sat down beside him at the pool and said, "Son, have you been saved?" Without hesitation he responded, "I've never drowned." My question related to salvation; his response related to his occupation. I quickly realized my mistake and began using language he would understand.

Law #4: The Law of the Lesson: *Truth that is taught must be learned through truth already known.*

The illustration of the lifeguard in the previous paragraph vividly proves this law. It is further verified by the teaching practices of Jesus. He was a master in using what His students already knew to teach them new truths. You have probably heard this statement about the Bible: The Old Testament is the New Testament concealed; the New Testament is the Old Testament revealed. Frequently Jesus explained this principle when His students would quote something from the Old Testament, or the Law. Jesus knew that His students had read the Law, but they didn't fully understand what it meant. To help them, Jesus would commend them for what they knew, but then lead them to things they didn't know.

In education, this is often referred to as sequential learning, or scope and sequences. Another word for it is epigenetic. Epigenetic learning, in its simplest form, means you master one level before going on to the next. It is illustrated in the life of an infant and in a child's progression through elementary school. Before infants can walk, they have to accomplish something else first. Typically, they have to learn to crawl. It's possible for some to bypass that step, but it's very unlikely they will walk until they have learned to hold their head up. In lower elementary education classes, you don't read *Gone With The Wind* or something from Shakespeare. You have to learn the ABCs first. You don't do algebra in the first grade either. You have to learn to count and recognize numbers before you learn to add and subtract. Apply this epigenetic principle, or scope and sequences, to spiritual truth. You have to learn some basic truths and even grow in spiritual maturity before you understand the deeper truths of the Bible. This may be expressed in different ways, but the concept is still true. Notice the words of the Apostle Paul when he says, "But the natural man (unbeliever) receiveth not the things of the Spirit of God: for they are foolishness unto him: neither can he know them, because they are spiritually discerned" (1 Corinthians 2:14). An even greater truth is taught when Jesus Himself said we must first come to Him in faith before we can know some things. In other words, faith comes before knowing.

Law #5: The Law of the Teaching Process: *The teacher must motivate and direct the self-activities of the learner.*

One of the greatest challenges every teacher faces is how to motivate students to learn. An even greater challenge is motivating students to want to learn on their own. Obviously, some information is best learned under the direction of a teacher, but the goal of any education is to motivate students to continue learning on their own. The challenge is no different for those of us who teach Bible and/or work in Christian education. Referring to this, Jonathan Thigpen stated: "(Teachers) do not merely impart knowledge but stimulate their students to acquire it."[7] He further suggested that teachers who want to help students learn to acquire knowledge on their own must:

1. Provide thoughtful material
2. Provoke investigation
3. Provide satisfaction

The research conducted by Whitaker and his staff certainly verifies that motivation in a classroom is of extreme importance. Note these concepts based on their research:[8]

1. Great teachers create a positive atmosphere each day in their classroom despite inevitable negatives such as irate parents, troubled students, and limited resources.

2. Effective teachers understand the power of praise and look for opportunities to find people doing things right.

3. To be effective, praise must be authentic, specific, immediate, clean, and private.

4. Effective teachers know that one of the most important tasks a teacher performs is to model appropriate behavior. Consequently, great

teachers model the behavior of treating people with dignity and respect all the time.

Law #6: The Law of the Learning Process: *The student must integrate into his or her own life the truth that has been taught.*

There is no greater accomplishment than learning something on your own. It's wonderful to have excellent teachers and mentors, but the greatest discovery of truth, or knowledge, is what you have gleaned yourself. It's helpful to have Bible commentaries, and other well-prepared materials to assist you in your teaching, but the easiest, and most enjoyable lessons you will ever teach are the ones you studied for and prepared on your own.

This concept is important in lesson preparation, but it's also a habit you need to impart to your students. Gathering knowledge for themselves is a skill that's probably better caught than taught. That is, when they see you enjoying what you're doing because you have discovered knowledge on your own, it leaves an impression on them. A good way to illustrate this to your students, particularly in Bible study, is by using three ideas: *observation, interpretation,* and *application.* This is often referred to as the inductive method of Bible study.

Observation

Select any passage of the Bible and read what it says. Be sure you fully understand each and every word. If there are words of which you don't know the meaning, look them up in a dictionary or even a Bible dictionary. It's important to know the meaning of every word in the passage. Don't go any further until you have accomplished this.

Interpretation

After observing the passage, find out what it means. What is the author saying? What does the author mean? At this point, it's good to even think about who said it, to whom the passage is stated, and the culture and time in which it is written. Get as much background information as you can. In other words, look for the meaning in the context of the section.

Application

Here is where the rubber meets the road and where too many Christians fall short in their personal Bible study. They think they know what a passage says. They even know facts about who said it, to whom it was said, the culture and background. All of that is well and good, but the real accomplishment comes when you make the application personal. Look at it like this:

- Observation: *what it says*
- Interpretation: *what it means*
- Application: *what it means **to me***

Law #7: The Law of Review and Application: *The teacher and student must continually review and apply the truth taught.*

The importance of this law is that it seeks to draw what has been taught in the past with what will be taught in the future. It's an attempt to show the relationship between what was taught in a previous lesson to what will be taught in an upcoming lesson. However, when you review a previous lesson, keep the following suggestions in mind:

1. Review only what has already been covered. Do not include new material in a review.

2. Keep it short—no more than 5-8 minutes.

It is also effective, once you have completed the review, to give a brief preview of what is to come. Doing this ties together what has already been presented with that which is yet to come. I remember years ago, when I taught the Gospel of John in a Bible college, reading a commentary that stated that John the Apostle was an excellent teacher because of the style of his writing. The commentator pointed out that the first chapter of John's Gospel was his introduction to the book. Chapters 2-19 told the story of the ministry of Jesus on earth, and chapters 20-21 tied everything together. But the commentator said John's approach was actually this: "I'm going to tell you what I'm going to tell you; I'm going to tell you; then, I'm going to tell you what I told you." That approach still works today in any teaching situation.

If you have been reading these laws carefully and comparing them to Whitaker's research, you see how relevant John Gregory's seven laws of teaching really are. They may be old, but they are still highly applicable.

For Further Discussion

1. Pick out one of Gregory's laws that appeals to you the most and decide what you need to do to make it personal.

2. Think about some practical expectations you could begin to incorporate in your Sunday School class.

3. Select a passage of the Bible to experiment with the inductive Bible study method of observation, interpretation, and application.

Notes

1. Teaching Techniques, Revitalizing Methodology, 2006 Edition, p. 16.

2. Study Guide, What Great Teachers Do Differently: 14 Things That Matter Most, p. 1

3. Teaching Techniques, Revitalizing Methodology, 2006, Edition, p. 17.

4. Study Guide, What Great Teachers Do Differently: 14 Things That Matter Most, p. 51.

5. Study Guide, What Great Teachers Do Differently: 14 Things That Matter Most, p. 7.

6. Teaching Techniques, Revitalizing Methodology, p. 18.

7. Teaching Techniques, Revitalizing Methodology, p. 19.

8. Study Guide, What Great Teachers Do Differently: 14 Things That Matter Most, p. 27.

Characteristics of Effective Teachers Personified

6

Throughout this book, mention has been made of one of the most recent forms of research on the elements of effective teaching. The research for the book, *What Great Teachers Do Differently: 14 Things That Matter Most*, was conducted by a team headed up by Todd Whitaker. The research lists the following fourteen truths about effective teaching:[1]

1. People are more important than programs.

2. Be willing to expect something from students.

3. Stop bad behavior before it starts.

4. Maintain high expectations for everyone, including yourself.

5. Teachers are the variables in the classroom and they should always improve.

6. A positive attitude, environment, and praise go a long way.

7. Take what you hear from students and teachers with a grain of salt.

8. Admit when something you've done didn't work or was just plain wrong.

9. Be willing to be flexible and adjust when necessary.

10. Challenge slower students to rise higher.

11. Challenge all students to rise higher.

12. Treat everyone as being good, even if they're not.

13. Keep standardized testing in its proper perspective.

14. Students don't care what you know until they know that you care.

When you look at the above list, it is to be admitted that some things may not apply to those of us who teach in Christian settings, but there are still many things that should be considered even then. Frankly, the only one that may not apply is number 13 regarding the use of standardized testing. All the others, however, should be carefully, and prayerfully, incorporated into your teaching ministry.

Chapters 1-4 presented five characteristics of the teaching ministry of Jesus Christ. When you add those five to at least thirteen of those presented by Whitaker, you have a total of eighteen characteristics of effective teachers. But there are more. Truthfully, there are probably as many effective characteristics as there are people who teach. That is oftentimes what qualifies as effective teaching depends upon the person making the evaluation. What is effective to some may be ineffective to others.

The teaching characteristics of Jesus are obviously from a biblical perspective. The characteristics from Todd Whitaker are based on academic research.

There is a third area that is more practical in nature, which will be discussed in the remainder of this chapter. These practical characteristics are actually based on qualities of some of the greatest teachers I was privileged to have as a student. In addition, as a college professor for many years, I have made it a practice to ask students what they think makes a teacher effective. Their thoughts are included as well. While each of the characteristics to be mentioned are actually personified in the life of individual people, no names or other means of identification will be given. The order in which they are presented has no significance whatsoever. They are simply listed to illustrate the influence of effective teaching.

Administrative Skills

Every teacher has to have administrative skills. In one sense, every teacher is the administrator of his or her subject matter and/or classroom. A lengthy discussion about the duties of an administrator is not necessary at this point, but keep in mind that the characteristic is essential.

Three such individuals personified this in my days of teacher preparation and ministry. One was a college president, one a pastor, and one a director of a Christian camp and conference center. The college president was a personal friend of my family. His oldest son and I attended rival high schools and often competed against each other. The administrative skills of this individual were many. However, it was not just his skills that impressed me. It was his appearance. I'm not sure what a college president looks like, but he looked like one. His appearance was always flawless. He looked "presidential." He was even one of my teachers, but even in that role you knew he was the leader of the college. He had a competent staff around him, but everyone always knew who was in charge. He was not arrogant but completely confident. When I had the fortune of being hired to work for him, he very quickly put me at ease. I was to head up a new division of the college that had never been offered. He said, "Kenneth, I really hope your experience here works out. I want to make you a promise. If the program succeeds, you'll get the credit. If it fails, I'll take the blame." How can you lose with that kind of support? I wanted to do well, but more important, he wanted me to do well. He knew what it meant to give people the opportunity to do their job. He knew how to delegate. I'm sure if I had done something out of line, he would have reprimanded me, but my relationship with him was always a good one. It's interesting that in Whitaker's research he mentions this very thing—having high expectations not only for your students but for yourself as well.

The other two administrators did not say the same exact things to me, but they knew the importance of delegation. They outlined my job to me, but they also allowed me the freedom to make it work with my abilities and personality. These three men reminded me of an important concept in the field of business: *It's amazing what can be accomplished when you don't care who gets the credit.* That needs to be revised for those of us in Christian education to "*It's amazing what can be accomplished if you give the Lord the credit.*" These three men did that.

Faith in God and Faith in Others

Students know if you like them or not. In fact, when students are afraid, or even intimidated, they don't learn as much. That doesn't mean teachers should be "buddy-buddy" and a "pal" but it does mean students need to feel appreciated. The person who demonstrated this to me was a rather large man. He would come to class and lecture without notes while he sat cross-legged on the desk. He used no visuals. He just lectured. It was a Saturday morning class in a secular university. Each week he would announce in advance what his lecture would be the following week. One particular Saturday he announced that his next lecture would be "Why I am a Christian and why I believe the Bible is true." Typically, people were absent from week to week, but on the day of this lecture, everyone attended. He told us his purpose for the lecture. "I'm speaking on this subject because if I don't, some of you will never hear the truth about Christ and the Bible." After his lecture, I made a point to thank him for his courage and tell him how it encouraged me to not be ashamed of my faith outside of the "religious arena." He expressed an appreciation for me that has stayed with me until this day. Again, Whitaker points out that students don't care how much you know until they know how much you care.

Commitment

Teachers who stay with it for several years do so because they enjoy what they're doing. One such teacher I was privileged to have made teaching a life-long ministry. He was committed not only to teaching but to the Bible, and nothing would deter him from that. One Christmas, this teacher presented me and other members of the college faculty with a copy of the *One Year Bible*. I have faithfully read it through every year. He also taught another important principle of commitment by saying that a preacher should be ready to preach, pray, or die at a moment's notice. I have made it a practice to have sermon outlines with me at all times because of his influence.

Courage

It may seem strange to say effective teachers need courage, but they do. They need courage to stand for truth in a dark, unsaved world. They need courage to stand for what they think is right, even against fellow Christians. While courage was certainly personified in this individual, an even greater impact was the attitude of humility he demonstrated towards those with whom there had been some disagreements. His humility would not allow him to be vindictive, even when events proved he was right. In the face of unkind criticism, he remained both humble and courageous and showed a spirit of love to those who had unduly belittled him.

Excellence

A speech teacher personified this attribute. Quite frankly, I didn't want to take speech at the college level. I had to take speech in elementary school because I had the physical conditions of a pronounced lisp, an oversized tongue, and teeth that did not meet. These problems caused me to have very low self-esteem. I didn't want to take speech because I never thought I'd be speaking in public. How could I be a public speaker with such physical problems? This teacher, however, saw something in me I didn't see in myself. One of her assignments for us was to build a poetry program on any topic and present it to the class. The idea was to select a topic, find several pieces of poetry on that topic, memorize it, and quote it for our classmates. It had to be done with proper pronunciation of the words, the feeling of the poets, and bodily expression. She would select the best presentations to be performed before the entire student body in a chapel setting. She demanded that it be as flawless as possible. All I wanted to do was get it over with. When I gave my presentation, she chose it as one of the presentations to be given in the chapel setting. I couldn't believe it! That experience bolstered my confidence and taught me that even with a lisp I could speak in public. I've been doing that now for a long time because a teacher made a demand, or expected something big from me. Again, this was one of the fourteen characteristics discovered by Todd Whitaker. How right he was.

Friendship

Having a teacher who becomes a lifelong friend is not only rare, it's a blessing. Earlier I made the observation that a teacher should not become a pal to the point that he or she steps down from the position of authority. Even so, being a friend to students can change their lives. This trait was personified to me by a music teacher. He taught me the mechanics of using my diaphragm when singing and speaking, how to direct a congregation in singing, and how to be a friend. Whatever the venue of singing, he was there to direct and give encouragement. It has now been over forty-five years and we still stay in touch. He honored me by naming a son after me.

Loyalty

Whatever the situation, a teacher needs to know that supervisors, or Sunday School superintendents, Christian education directors, and/or pastors are there for them. Teachers need to know that those who have appointed them to teach are behind them. Too often Christian teachers in church settings are left on their own, and sometimes such teachers need someone in whom they can confide. Unfortunately, too few teachers in church settings are praised and given the recognition and appreciation they deserve. If you are responsible for supervising a group of teachers, show your support and loyalty to them. It will increase the effectiveness of both the individual teacher and the total ministry.

Love

In one sense, all the attributes of effective teaching are based on love. Love is one of those words that is often better demonstrated than defined. The reality is that there are some people who display love better than others. The personification of this trait is easy for me to mention and even though I stated earlier I would not identify any particular person, I must do so here. My father was the personification of love. As a denominational leader, he developed that reputation. As a minister of the Gospel, he was known for his love for both believers and unbelievers. One friend even said to me, "If I ever backslide, I want Raymond Riggs to give the invitation to return, because I'm sure I'll repent and come back to the Lord." Daddy had the ability to love people regardless of skin color, social status, denominational affiliation or lack of it, and/or differences in theology. Having love does not mean you're a wimp or a pushover. He was neither of those. He knew how to stand firm and yet still love you. He knew how to disagree without being disagreeable.

If you've been keeping count of all the characteristics of effective teachers, you have probably noticed it's a lengthy list. It totals twenty-seven characteristics in all. As a reminder, read them again:

Characteristics of Jesus Christ

1. He demonstrated what He said.

2. He desired to serve.

3. He was discerning of His students.

4. He was dedicated to the Scriptures.

5. He was diverse in His situations.

What Great Teachers Do Differently (Todd Whitaker)

6. People are more important than programs.

7. Be willing to expect something from students.

8. Stop bad behavior before it starts.

9. High expectations should be for everyone, including the teacher.

10. Teachers are the variables in the classroom and they should always improve.

11. A positive attitude, environment, and praise go a long way.

12. Take what you hear from students and teachers with a grain of salt.

13. Admit when something you've done didn't work or was just plain wrong.

14. Be willing to be flexible and adjust when necessary.

15. Challenge slower students to rise higher.

16. Challenge all students to rise higher.

17. Treat everyone as being good, even if they're not.

18. Keep standardized testing in its proper perspective.

19. Students don't care what you know until they know that you care.

Attributes Personified

20. Administrative skills

21. Faith in God and faith in others

22. Commitment

23. Courage

24. Excellence

25. Friendship

26. Loyalty

27. Love

Quite frankly, that's a tall order for any teacher. You could probably find many more attributes by making your own list. No doubt just a casual visit to a local bookstore, browsing what's available, would give you even more. Here's the point: the effectiveness of a teacher often depends upon each student's personal experience with a particular teacher. A good teacher to some may not be to others, but the challenge is great. Every teacher should constantly be striving to be the absolute best.

Ask your students what they think about effective teachers. Typically, I ask these two questions of teacher education students: (1) Why do you want to be a teacher, and (2) What do you remember about teachers you've had in the past? The answers are very revealing. To the first question, the responses have included, but are not limited to, the following:

1. I like learning and want to teach others.

2. I remember a teacher who had a big influence in my life.

3. I want to help someone like another teacher helped me in the past.

The responses to the second question are equally revealing:

1. They were very patient with me.

2. They made things easy to understand.

3. They took a personal interest in me.

4. They acted like they really cared about me.

What is of interest about the above responses is that seldom, if ever, do they relate to where teachers have gone to college or what kind of degree they attained. It's not how much knowledge a teacher has or what honors they received. Yes, teachers should be qualified and trained as much as possible, but sometimes those factors are more important to others than they are to the actual students in the classrooms. Students may or may not remember much about the subject matter they were taught, but they definitely remember what they liked and didn't like about the teacher.

For Discussion

1.   Think back in your experience of being a student. Which teachers do you remember? Why do you remember them? What were their good traits? What were their bad traits?

2.   Look at Whitaker's fourteen things and compare them to teachers you have had in the past. How many of these traits did your teachers have?

3.   Discuss with your students the concept that teachers need to be cautious about being too friendly with students. Can it actually present problems?

4.   Create your own list of effective teacher qualifications. (That is, what are some other characteristics not listed in this chapter that you may have observed in some of your teachers?)

Notes

1. Whitaker, Todd and Beth. Study Guide, *What Great Teachers Do Differently: 14 Things that Matter Most.* Eye on Education, 2006. 75.

Two Essential Ingredients of Effective Teaching

7

If you are familiar with the Boy Scouts of America, you may recognize the famous slogan, "be prepared." Those two words are more than a slogan. They are the Boy Scouts' motto. The founder of Boy Scouts, Baden Powell, was asked on one occasion, "Be prepared for what?" His response was, "Why, for any old thing. The training you receive in your troop will help you live up to the Scout motto. When someone has an accident, you are prepared because of your first aid instruction. Because of the lifesaving practice, you might be able to save a non-swimmer who has fallen into deep water. Be prepared for life—to live happily and without regret, knowing that you have done your best. That's what the Scout motto means."[1] But Baden Powell wasn't thinking just of being ready for emergencies. His idea was that all Scouts should prepare themselves to become productive citizens and to give happiness to other people. He wanted each Scout to be ready in mind and body for any struggles and to meet with a strong heart whatever challenges might lie ahead.

Obviously, the motto prescribed by Baden Powell is a lofty one. Those of us who teach spiritual truth and Biblical knowledge should seek to have the same attitude. Unfortunately, too often the following scenario takes place when it comes to teaching:

- You all pray for me today. I didn't know I was supposed to teach.
- Brother Stanley, you read the first verse and tell us what it means.
- Brother Stanley reads the verse and says, "It means what it says."
- Thank you. Now someone else read the next verse.

This particular scene has been duplicated too many times in too many church settings. It's ironic that people who say they believe the Bible often treat it so haphazardly when it comes time to teach it. If we believe the Bible like we say we do, why is so much of our teaching bland and ineffective?

There are two key ingredients in teaching, regardless of the subject matter. The age level, the curriculum, or the situation make no difference—the ingredients are the same. These two ingredients are preparation and presentation.

Preparation

In all areas of life, preparation is vital. We expect it in fields like medicine and law. None of us would knowingly agree to surgery if we knew the surgeon was unprepared, or even ill-prepared. We want to be sure the mechanic who services our vehicles knows what he is doing. If we need a lawyer, we want one who knows the law well. In the field of education, we expect those who teach our children to be trained in educational procedures. We want the best teachers we can get. We want them to be qualified, certified, and have the proper licensing. And rightly we should. But why is it when it comes to teaching the Bible we somehow take a different approach? Why is it that Sunday School teachers are not required to meet some kind of standard before they teach? This is not to say that all of those who are teaching in churches today are ineffective, but many are woefully lacking in training, knowledge, and preparation. Neither is this to say that all teachers in church need to have Bible college training, but too often they have no training at all.

Preparation, while it may involve a formalized approach, is basically personal. It is the time a teacher spends getting ready to teach. At least three areas of preparation should be considered: (1) preparation of yourself; (2) preparation of the content of the lesson; and (3) preparation of the classroom.

Preparation of Yourself

Every aspect of yourself is involved in teaching. This is true regardless of the level you teach. Teaching involves physical, emotional, social, intellectual, and spiritual preparation. Each of these areas must be prepared if teaching is to be effective. The amount of rest you get on Saturday night will make a difference in your effectiveness on Sunday morning. How you relate to others in your classroom may very well hinge on how you feel physically. What you have learned, or haven't learned, as you studied the lesson will be obvious. It's been said, "Don't tell people you're not prepared to teach. They'll know it." The type of preparation that is needed to be effective cannot be accomplished in a few minutes; it's a process that becomes a part of your personality.

One well-known Bible scholar and writer of commentaries was asked, "How do you get so much out of just one verse or phrase of the Bible?" His response was somewhat shocking. "It has nothing to do with brain power. It has to do with staying still long enough until I'm sure I understand what is being said." His point should be well taken by every teacher: preparation takes time. Preparing yourself involves getting ready the night before. It may seem trivial, and maybe even ridiculous, but knowing before you go to bed what you're going to wear the next morning cuts down on a lot of frustration. Not finding what you want to wear can put your mind in a different gear and cause your attitude to be on edge. Having to look for socks or iron a shirt at the last minute may not seem to have spiritual implications, but your spiritual attitude can be greatly affected by these little things.

Preparation of the Content of the Lesson

How you study a particular passage involves your preferences and learning habits. There are many good methods of Bible study, but no method is more important than your personal desire and attitude. You should *want* to prepare; you should *want* to give a good presentation. This kind of preparation takes time. It is an ongoing activity instead of a last-minute affair. It begins long before the Saturday night before the lesson is to be taught. Reading the lesson well in advance gives your mind the opportunity to meditate and think. As you prepare yourself to know the content, your mind will begin to think of various ways, or methods, to best teach that truth. Understanding the background of a passage makes it clearer to you and consequently makes it more enjoyable for your students.

Preparation of the Classroom

Your classroom may already be determined and in some cases, you may not even have a choice regarding the type of room it is. You may be forced to use a small room with poor lighting, but there are still some things you can do to make it a place conducive to effective teaching. Ask yourself these questions: What does the room look like? Is it colorful or drab? Is it dirty or clean? Could the lighting be changed without a lot of expense? Are the chairs appropriate to the age of the students? Would tables be better? Would it be convenient to rearrange the chairs if necessary? Every teacher in public and private schools has a planning period to deal with these kinds of questions. Your planning may need to be done at home, but don't wait until the day of the lesson to begin that planning.

Presentation

The greater the preparation, the greater the presentation. Effective preparation makes the presentation more enjoyable for both the teacher and the students. This aspect of the teaching process is where the rubber meets the road. All the preparation now becomes presentation. The presentation is actually an overflow of your preparation. Presentation involves your methods and materials, the use of your voice, and your enthusiasm. It's our preparation on display. The day is gone when you can stand in front of a class with a teacher's manual in your hand or have someone read aloud for you from their printed material. The Bible deserves much more than that. The presentation of your material should have the following three aspects: enthusiasm, variety, and expectations for the students.

Be Enthusiastic

Enthusiasm is contagious. When the teacher is excited about the class, the students sense it. Enthusiasm is based on what you have personally gleaned from your preparation. The key to enthusiasm is being genuine. It's the kind of enthusiasm that springs from learning something that you might not have known before as you look at a passage of Scripture. It's an attitude of wanting to share with others what you have discovered so they can discover it as well. A good example of this appears in the book of Luke. Our Lord was traveling with His disciples, and He used the opportunity to teach them some spiritual truths they had not previously known. Luke talks about it in Luke 24:27–35. As the disciples walked along with the Lord, He shed light on the darkness of their spiritual minds regarding His own purpose for coming to earth. Luke states it like this: "And beginning at Moses and all the prophets, he expounded unto them in all the scriptures the things concerning himself" (Luke 24:27). Further on, Luke shares their reaction: "And their eyes were opened, and they knew him; ...and they said to one another, Did not our heart burn within us, while he talked with us by the way, and while he opened to us the scriptures?...and they told what things were done in the way, and how he was known of them in breaking of bread" (Luke 24:31–32, 35).

When you read that, you get a picture of excitement. They discerned things they had never known ("...their eyes were opened...") and they were excited about what they had learned ("...did not our hearts burn within us...") and they had to share it with others ("...they told what things were done in the way..."). This is not to imply that you can have the same impact on your students as the Lord had on His, but on the other hand, maybe we can, since we are invited to "...let this mind be in you which was also in Christ Jesus..." (Philippians 2:5). When you prepare and rely on the power of the Holy Spirit to assist you in imparting truth, it does make an impact on those you teach.

Do Something Different

Instead of using the same approach or method over and over, do something different. Rearrange the room. Make use of appropriate visuals or other forms of media. Have a discussion. Involve members of the class with the teaching; don't be the only one who talks. Take a fieldtrip. Utilize the abilities of those in your class who may have knowledge of things you don't know as much about. Spice things up.

Expect Something from the Class

"Wait a minute. I have a hard enough time just getting them to class. How can I set expectations for them?" Is it possible that the reason some of them do not come is that nothing is expected from them? (Don't forget that one of Todd Whitaker's research findings is that effective teachers expect something from students.) Nothing motivates learning like learning something you didn't know before. It's simply an educational fact that students only rise as high as the teacher's demands. For example, when you ask a question, expect an answer. Don't answer for them. Learn to "wait them out." The silence will soon become boring and before long someone will break the silence and give an answer. Ask a question that requires more than just a "yes" or "no" response. Ask something that requires more than just a nod of the head in agreement with you. Don't be afraid to have disagreements. Obviously, you want to keep the class civil and polite, but differences of opinions can be beneficial.

Don't be afraid to say there are some things in the Bible you don't fully understand. It's not wrong to have questions. In fact, having questions prompts learning. When you come to a passage that you're not sure about, highlight it, or mark it somehow in your Bible. Begin to search for answers and refuse to give up until your mind is satisfied, and then you'll be teaching your students by example to do the same. To get you started, and to illustrate this point, notice the following:

1. When God told Elijah to pour water on the sacrifice, it hadn't rained for three years. Where did Elijah get the water? (1 Kings 18:17–41)

2. When Jesus cursed the fig tree, it withered and died, but one Bible writer says it wasn't time for the figs. Why did Jesus curse a fig tree for not having figs when it wasn't time to have figs? (Mark 11:12–14)

3. When God became angry with Moses and wanted to kill him, what was God angry about? Why did He want to kill Moses? (Exodus 4:24)

4. Was Judas a Christian? If he wasn't, why did the Lord allow him to be in his band of disciples?

5. It might be speculative, but have a discussion regarding how Mary, the mother of the Lord, must have felt when the angel told her she would give birth in a supernatural way. How did *her* mother feel? How did Joseph feel? (Matthew 1:18–25)

Don't forget that even one of the Lord's disciples, Thomas, had his doubts, and the Lord encouraged him to find the truth for himself. Finding the answer to the above questions, and many more, actually strengthens your faith. When you have a desire to know the answers, that desire motivates you to keep learning. Jesus was a master teacher, and as such, He knew the importance of an effective presentation. Study His life carefully. Granted, He was God in the flesh, but He always practiced good educational principles in His teaching. He was always aware of His audience or students. He expected something from them. He used methods that were common in His day.

One final thought about expecting something from your students. Did not the Lord make demands of His disciples? Does He not make demands of us as well? If you've forgotten that truth, go back and read the Old Testament. Over and over Moses reminded the people when he gave them the laws of God that God's demand was to obey. Disobedience carried stiff penalties and consequences. The New Testament teaches the same truth. Jesus taught that believers are to be obedient. Many New Testament writers echo His teaching. James puts it very clearly: "But be ye doers of the word, and not hearers only, deceiving your own selves" (James 1:22). That's expectation.

For Further Discussion

1. Take note of the teaching methods of Jesus. Some are as follows:

    a. Object lessons; familiarity (Luke 5:1–11; 20:21–26)

    b. Reasoning; provoking (Luke 5:17–26)

    c. Lecture; application (Luke 6:20–38)

    d. Small group; away from others (Luke 9:1–10)

    e. Partner; experience (Luke 10:1–23)

    f. Question; discussion (Luke 18:18–30)

    g. Question; thinking (Luke 20:21–26)

2. Invite your class to mention other Scripture passages of which they may have had doubts.

3. Invite your class to share how they came to understand a spiritual truth they had wondered about in the past.

Notes

1. Boy Scout Handbook, 11th Edition, 1998. 54.

Understanding Psychology

8

When you hear or read the word "psychology," what comes to your mind? Often a negative thought is all people have. They have heard that psychology is something mysterious or even demonic, and certainly not something Christians should study. Such an attitude is unfortunate. By definition, psychology is the systematic, scientific study of behaviors and mental processes. Three things need to be clearly understood. First, psychology deals with behavior. It is the study of a person's observable actions or responses. Secondly, it deals with the mental processes or what goes on in a person's mind such as thinking, planning, and imagination. Thirdly, psychology is the study of the psyche. Look at the word again: psychology. It comes from two different words—psyche and logos. Psyche simply refers to the individual. Logos means word. Therefore, psychology is the word of the psyche, or the study of the individual.

Another way to understand psychology is to be aware of what it seeks to do, or its purpose. Typically, psychology has four goals: (1) to describe that organisms behave in certain ways; (2) to explain the causes of that behavior; (3) to predict future behavior; and (4) to control behavior. These four goals are the driving force behind all psychology. When you look at these goals, and properly understand them, you'll see they are no different than some of the aspects of our spiritual growth. Take the four goals of psychology and lay them beside Christian truth and you'll get the point.

Psychological Goal	Spiritual Truth
Describe behavior	Born into sin (Romans 5:12)
Explain behavior	Sinful by nature (Romans 6:23)
Predict future behavior	Become a new creature (2 Corinthians 5:17)
Control behavior	Work of the Holy Spirit (John 16:13)

Psychology is an attempt to help us understand people better. It is not above Scripture, but when properly understood, it gives us valuable tools that enhance our teaching. As believers who trust in the accuracy of the Bible, we understand that people are sinners because the Bible says this. It is one of the basic teachings of the Bible. People became sinners because of the sin of Adam and Eve (Romans 5:12 and 6:23). People behave like they do because they have a sinful nature. We describe them as sinners because sin is an inherently human trait. However, the great advantage of Christianity over psychology is the fact that when individuals repent and accept Christ as Savior, their behavior changes and they are given the indwelling of the Holy Spirit to guide them into new truth.

Because of the variety of factors affecting human behavior, professionals have developed different methods that focus on specific aspects of psychology.

Psychobiological Psychology
Psychobiology refers to the study of how the physical body interacts with an environment and how that environment influences learning and personality development.

Cognitive Psychology
Cognitive psychology refers to how we learn, process information, store information, and retrieve information stored in the brain. This part of cognitive development is called the academic domain, or knowledge domain. Another part of cognitive development is the affective domain, or how we feel. These two are directly related. That is, how you feel can determine how well you learn. One is the emotional aspect; the other is the knowledge aspect.

Behavioral Psychology
The behavioral aspect of psychology refers to how a person's behavior may be modified through a process of either rewards and/or punishments. This is often called behavior modification. Remember, two of the goals of psychology are to predict and control a person's behavior.

Psychoanalytic Psychology
This is the more technical side of psychology. It deals with how the personality and behavior are influenced by unconscious experiences. It is this type of psychology that oftentimes Christians shy away from but the simple truth is, even Christians behave in ways that are based on past experiences.

Humanistic Psychology
Another less practical approach to psychology is known as humanistic psychology. This refers to how a person's personal freedom, creativity, and potential influence his or her behavior. It's another way of saying that people are different. Being different is not a foreign concept to Christianity. Quite the contrary. The gifts of the Holy Spirit are actually designed around this concept. Reread the passages that deal with the gifts of the spirit and you will see that differences in people are actually an advantage. (Those passages are: Ephesians 4:11–16; Romans 12:3–8; 1 Corinthians 12:1–30.)

Cross-Cultural Psychology

This type of psychology is one of the more interesting because it deals with how culture and ethnic factors influence behavior and how people are both similar and different. If you have ever read the Bible all the way through, you are aware that this approach is described in many places. You see it in such places as the Old Testament, when Moses warned the Children of Israel against becoming like the foreign nations around them. You see it in the writings of Paul, when he talked about the impact of hanging on to the old way of the Jewish laws instead of embracing the liberty found in Christ.

Eclectic Psychology

An eclectic view refers to selecting from or using various ideas and/or methods of observation to study a person's behavior. It is a combination of different approaches.

Sometimes people get confused about the difference between a psychologist, a clinical psychologist, and a psychiatrist. The differences, in a simplistic explanation, are these:

Psychologist

A psychologist is trained in the fields of education and psychology. The training in education deals with some of the areas of psychology such as cognitive development (how people learn), classroom management, methods of teaching, etc. The psychological aspect of training revolves around understanding how the mind and brain function. Often a psychologist becomes a counselor in a professional sense, actually hanging out a "shingle" advertising their availability. These professionals may even serve in a school setting as a guidance counselor.

Clinical Psychologist

A clinical psychologist has an advanced education in psychology with an emphasis on diagnosing and treating abnormal behavior. Such an individual may have a career in a hospital working with patients confined to a mental ward. He or she may even work with law enforcement in dealing with criminals.

Psychiatrist

The basic difference in the psychiatrist and the psychologist is the fact that training in psychiatry also includes medical training in addition to other areas of education and psychology. A psychiatrist may subscribe medicine where the psychologist cannot.

Another way to understand psychology is to be aware of the different specializations within psychology. It is not possible to list every area nor to give a lengthy explanation of the ones presented, but psychology in its diversity includes the following:

Social Psychology
Social psychology deals with the social interactions, cultures, group behaviors, and ethnic differences.

Personality Psychology
Personal psychology deals with the development of the personality as well as changes in the personality and its causes. It also involves assessments of the personality through a series of tests.

Developmental Psychology
This area is much broader in that it deals with the areas of moral, social, emotional, physical, and cognitive development. It is sometimes referred to as life span psychology or even physiological psychology because it deals with human development from conception to death and the development of an individual during a lifetime.

Experimental Psychology
Experimental psychology is the research aspect of the field. Psychological research may involve studying not just individuals, but groups of people and ethnic backgrounds from around the world.

Psychometrics
Psychometrics deals with testing skills, achievement tests, and IQ evaluations. Such a discipline not only administers standardized tests but also seeks to understand and interpret the various test results.

To further understand what psychology is all about, notice some other questions that psychology seeks to answer:

1. Is it really possible to control another individual?

2. If it's possible to control others, what are some ways to control them?

3. To what extent can you be controlled without even knowing it?

4. How much do we really understand others? Ourselves?

5. Where do we see the impact of psychology in everyday life?

6. What is normal? What is crazy?

Earlier in this chapter, psychology is defined in somewhat of a textbook fashion. Look at the definition of it in a more practical sense. Psychology is the exploration of the mysteries and marvels of human existence. It seeks to understand the vast and varied realm of human behavior. It involves the working of the body and the brain. It evaluates the way humans resemble each other and how they differ. Psychology is the study of what makes humans tick. Note the words *mysteries, marvels, vast, varied, body, brain, resemble, differ,* and *tick.* Each of these words shows what psychology is all about. Psychology is an attempt to see how each of these words relate and even interact with the development of the human psyche.

Psychology may be understood by recognizing that it overlaps with other subjects, such as philosophy, religion, physiology, anthropology, and sociology, to name a few. This overlap reveals just how important it is to know as much about individuals as possible before you can truly say you understand them. Each of the subjects is a study within itself, but when you link it with psychology, it enhances understanding even more. The dictionary defines these words individually.

Philosophy

This is the study of beliefs regarding God, existence, conduct, and man's relation with the universe. It involves the values of an individual and what each individual thinks is important.

Religion

Religion is a worldview and set of beliefs that answer the basic questions about life. It often recognizes a supreme being as an object of worship.

Physiology

This is a science that deals with the functions and processes of life including plants, animals, and human beings. In psychology it overlaps with the physical development and the various stages of growth that every human experiences. In short, physiology is the study of how things grow and what forces and influences cause this growth.

Anthropology

The dictionary states this is the study of every aspect of mankind as humans. It involves areas such as the physical and social aspects of man's development.

Sociology

This is a science that deals with the origin, development, and nature of problems confronting society. It also involves various aspects of relationships that humans experience with others, including culture, language, lifestyles, differences, and similarities.

The point of all of this is this: You cannot and do not fully understand individuals by only looking at one aspect of their life. Humans are a composite of everything and everyone that has ever influenced them even in the smallest of ways. Understanding individuals involves being aware of some basic psychological principles and factors, such as:

1. A person's behavior is fickle, which means it's not always predictable.

2. Understanding a person's behavior involves knowing things like:

   a. Sense organs, or parts of a human's make-up that are observable and

   b. Visceral organs, or parts of a human's make-up that are not observable, such as feelings.

3. The relationship between the brain and the body:

   a. Are men and women different in which side of the brain they use?

   b. Is it really possible to be left-brained or right-brained?

4. Heredity elements play a role.

5. Environmental elements also affect a person. These include:

   a. Physical environment

   b. Cultural environment

6. The actions of others, such as peer pressure, influence and shape individuals.

In reality, each of these interacts with the others in giving a better understanding of a human being. It must be understood that humans should be understood as a whole person, not just in individual parts.

For Further Discussion

1. What is your personal definition of psychology?

2. Review the four goals of psychology and evaluate how they may be useful to you as a Christian.

3. What are the various approaches in studying psychology today?

4. Review the differences in a psychologist, a clinical psychologist, and a psychiatrist.

5. In your own opinion, list four reasons a Christian should have a knowledge of psychology.

6. Review the seven basic psychological principles that are involved in truly understanding another individual. Which one(s) do you think is/are more important?

What is Educational Psychology?

9

As a Christian educator, I have been asked at times why a Christian would be interested in the secular field of psychology. Why would a Christian want to teach such a subject, particularly on a secular campus? Quite frankly, my answer is, "Why not?" I don't understand why some people would consider the area of psychology off limits for a Christian. By definition, psychology is the science that studies the human mind and behavior. What is it about that definition that would even prompt someone to ask why a Christian would be involved in psychology? A psychology textbook may expand on that by stating that psychology is the scientific study of the organisms, or the study of how living creatures are able to interact with their environment and each other, or (in its simplest form) understanding what makes humanity tick. Psychology could even be expanded to say that it overlaps with other sciences like sociology, anthropology, physiology, and religion. But again, why would these things prohibit a Christian from having a career in psychology?

Psychology is more than a curriculum. It's a way of thinking. You see it in politics, advertising, education, the media, religion, and relationships. It's a matter of seeking to understand the behaviors and mental processes of people. All of that should be a concern for the Christian educator as well. Browse through the following descriptions of psychology and you should notice that a thorough grasp of psychology will make you a more effective teacher.

- A discipline that is concerned with the teaching and learning process

- A discipline that seeks to determine what good teaching is

- The study of development, learning, and motivation in any type of school setting

Another way to define it may best be seen by the goals of educational psychology:
- To understand and improve the teaching/learning process

- To develop knowledge and methods of teaching

- To study learning and teaching in every teaching situation

- To examine what happens when <u>someone</u> teaches <u>something</u> to <u>someone else</u>

For the believer in general, and the Christian educator in particular, psychology helps us understand people. As Christians we should approach psychology as being inferior to Christianity but, properly understood, psychology can be of tremendous help. Consider the following:

- Psychology and Christianity provide information for daily living.

- Psychology and Christianity suggest ways for individuals to be responsible citizens.

- Psychology and Christianity give ideas and methods of how to be better people on the job, and in the family.

- Psychology and Christianity teach the necessity of developing individuals to be the very best in all areas of life.

- Psychology and Christianity provide information about what to expect in human growth and development.

Every Christian teacher of any Christian education venue should be interested in all of the above definitions and goals, even more so than secular educators. Christian education by its own name exists to honor Christ and the Bible clearly teaches that Christians should excel in everything they do—not for their own glory, but for the glory of Christ.

Students in psychology learn that human growth and development are influenced by multi-directional, multi-contextual, multi-cultural, multi-disciplinary, and plasticity factors. That is, the human body and mind are a complex entity. To understand the behavior of mankind, you have to look at more than one aspect. You have to look at every aspect of a person's life to fully understand why they are the way they are. Understanding a person's behavior and mental processes begins with the kind of birth he or she experienced. Were there any complications? Was the person born prematurely? What was their birth order in the family? What about the genetic makeup? What about their culture?

A host of other questions could be listed, but the point is psychology and Christianity provide answers and let us know that growth and development are a normal process of life. Humans are physical, social, emotional, psychological, and spiritual creatures. It's interesting to note that in the description of our Lord in Luke's account (Luke 2:52), with the exception of a psychological aspect, Jesus is described as a physical, social, emotional, and spiritual individual. Look at His life closely. Jesus increased: He continued to develop; He had wisdom: intellect and common sense; He had a certain stature: physical growth; He experienced favor with God and with man:

spiritual and social maturity. In His ministry you see His emotional side when He cried, had compassion, and displayed anger and frustration.

Yes, there are vast differences between psychology and Christianity and when you understand those differences, Christianity will always come out on top but that doesn't mean Christians cannot benefit from knowing something about psychology. Some of the differences between Christianity and psychology are as follows:

- Christianity is based on the premise that all truth is God's truth.

- Christianity believes in absolutes, or the fact that truth can be known.

- Christianity believes the ultimate source of truth is found only in God.

- Christianity believes that truth may be found in divine creation and Scripture.

- Psychology cannot explain the purpose of human existence nor the meaning of life on earth.

- Psychology cannot offer any hope for life after death.

- Psychology cannot offer any real comfort in times of tragedy and grief.

- Psychological truth is not on the same level with the truth of Scripture.

Christianity ranks above psychology because it has better answers. When psychology says that humans do what they do because of being mistreated or having a bad environment, Christianity says humans do what they do because they're sinful. Psychology seeks to change a person's environment and culture; Christianity seeks to change a person's character. Psychology has no hope to offer in this life or the life to come. Christianity offers hope for both. Psychology says that humans are basically good. Christianity does recognize that even sinful people have a quality of goodness, yet it also states that everyone is depraved and in need of redemption.

Further evidence of Christianity and educational psychology may be seen in two facts of history. Unfortunately, these two facts of history have been forgotten, if even known by some, but they verify that good educational principles and Christianity can have long-lasting results.

The Old Deluder Satan Act of 1647

This is almost completely forgotten in the history texts of today. Whether or not the neglect of this piece of history has been intentional cannot be proven, but those of us who teach in the field of Christian education should never forget it. The idea of this law came from the mind of the early colonists not long after coming to America from England. It stated that any town of fifty households was to hire a teacher. The teacher was to be paid a salary by the parents in the town. One of the main purposes of the law was to teach reading to the children so they in turn could read the Bible "...ere the old deluder Satan..." would captivate their minds. A town that did not start such a school could be fined. It is thought by many that our expression "an idle mind is the devil's workshop" may have come from this law. However, there were some parents who found it was cheaper to pay the fine than to start a school and pay a teacher. In many cases, such schools were started under the jurisdiction of a church. You are encouraged to either look in an old encyclopedia or simply go to Google and type in Old Deluder Satan Act of 1647 to read further details and the original wording of this law.

The Sunday School Movement of 1780

This is another important historical aspect in Christian education that influenced public education. While others had started the idea, it became popularized in Gloucester, England, under the direction of a local printer by the name of Robert Raikes. For several years, Mr. Raikes had been involved with prison reform by visiting adult prisons in an attempt to rehabilitate the prisoners. Later, he realized it would be easier to reach children before they became adults rather than trying to reform them later. With the help of a lady by the name of Mrs. Meredith, he began to go through his hometown and invite children off the streets to her home to have school. There were no child labor laws and children worked six days per week in the local factories, but on Sundays they were free to roam the streets. He gathered as many children as he could find and took them to Mrs. Meredith's kitchen where he taught them "reading, 'rithmetic, 'ritin, and religion." It was not without opposition from those who felt he was making a mockery of Sunday, but soon the idea caught on and other such schools were formed. They were not Sunday Schools in the way we understand them, however. They were schools that met on Sunday for six to eight hours with more than just religious curriculum. It was one of the first attempts to educate the poor and needy. Previously, education was only for the privileged. The purpose of schools like this was to teach some form of education that included religion. Again, you can read far more by going to Google and typing in Robert Raikes and the Sunday School Movement.

These two historical events illustrate that education and some form of religious instruction go together. Time does not allow for more details, but you should also learn about the importance of a Hornbook and the New England Primer as being two attempts to provide some form of curriculum for students.

Cognitive Development

Educational Psychology deals with a variety of topics but among the most important is the concept of cognitive development. Cognitive development refers to knowledge and how people make sense of and remember information and ideas. It is a study of how the brain works in receiving information or data, how the brain catalogs information, and how that information is recalled. Cognitive development further deals with how people of different ages go through that process. It is different for children than it is for adolescents and adults. Understanding is the result of a cognitive process that is more than merely memorizing and/or retelling something in your own words. In other words, memorizing Scripture does not mean the individual has learned the meaning of the Scriptures. Christian teachers want students to know the meaning of what they have memorized, and having an understanding of the principles of educational psychology can help you motivate students to do that.

Cognitive development deals with the fact that people learn differently. That's not news for those of us in Christian education. Teaching biblical truth does not change the process of education.

One of the leading professionals in the field of cognitive development was a Frenchman by the name of Jean Piaget. He devised four stages that he believed children go through as they begin the process of learning. While Mr. Piaget originally gave age limits for each of his stages, it is thought today that those age limitations may not be appropriate because it's possible to use all stages at different ages of an individual's life. As an effective teacher, it's good to know those stages because it can help you understand the mindset of your students. His four stages, with his original age limits and a brief explanation, are presented below:

• *Sensorimotor, birth to about age 2*

Sensorimotor actually refers to two elements that assist this age child in his cognitive development. They are the senses and the bodily movement of the arms, hands, legs, and feet. According to Piaget, a child learns by putting things into his mouth. It's the child's natural reaction to curiosity during this phase of learning. This way he finds out how things taste on the tongue, how they smell, how they feel in his hands, what they look like, and what they sound like. The body movement operates by putting items in the mouth.

• Preoperational, ages 2-6 years

In this stage of cognitive development, children are egocentric. Egocentric, says Piaget, refers to the fact that a child is not even aware that another opinion other than his own even exists. During this time a child is very imaginative as well, which is good for their thinking skills. Other terms associated with this age are object permanence and conservation. Object permanence refers to what Piaget believed regarding a child's mind in that if a child cannot see an object, it no longer exists. It's what is sometimes referred to as "out of sight, out of mind." Conservation refers to the idea that changing the shape of something does not change its substance. For instance, older children and adults are aware that a dollar can be a dollar bill, four quarters, ten dimes, twenty nickels, or 100 pennies. But to a child, 100 pennies is more than a dollar because there are more objects to hold in his hand.

• Concrete operational, 6-11 years of age

Basically, this is a period when a child's thinking is in literal terms. Children have a tendency to believe anything and everything you tell them. That's good to a point, but they have not as yet learned that some things are abstract or hypothetical. As they get closer to age 11, they're beginning to recognize that difference.

• Formal operational, from age 12 through adulthood

According to Piaget, formal operational is the final stage of cognitive development and continues on throughout the rest of a person's life. It is the process by which we continue to learn new information, process it, store it in the brain, and recall it back as needed. What you need to be aware of is the fact the many cognitive theorists today believe that Piaget's stages, while valuable, may not be as rigid as previously thought. This is particularly true in some of the younger stages, such as the sensorimotor stage. In Piaget's original thoughts, it was almost as if a child no longer used a stage of development after aging out of it and reaching the next stage. That is just not the case. For instance, Piaget is correct by stating that children from birth to age two learn things by putting objects in their mouth, but they do not stop doing that when they reach age three or even beyond. Even adults put things in their mouth to see what something tastes like. Watch them at a buffet to verify that. If they taste something and decide they don't like it, they don't take it, but they have used their senses to make that decision. Other areas of Piaget's theory may also be less rigid in reality as well.

You may not have an interest in all aspects of psychology, but as a teacher you should know the basic stages of development, particularly for the age of the students you teach. You will be more effective when you understand that children learn differently from adolescents, and adolescents learn differently from adults. Knowing something about the physical, emotional, social, and psychological development of your students makes you a more effective teacher.

One of the most helpful resources for understanding the meaning of educational psychology from a Christian perspective has been developed by William R. Yount. In his book, *Created To Learn*, he has developed what he calls The Disciplers' Model and Educational Psychology. "The Model consists of seven elements that exist, ideally in balanced tension." [1] The Model is actually a picture of a building inside a circle in which each part of the building and circle represents an educational psychology principle. Those seven principals are: (1) the Bible; (2) the needs of learners; (3) helping learners think; (4) helping learners relate; (5) helping learners value; (6) growth; and (7) the Holy Spirit. In outline form, the explanation of the model is as follows:

1. The left foundation stone: the Bible

    a. Divinely inspired (2 Timothy 3:16; 2 Peter 1:21)

    b. Sacred

        i. Don't take away from, nor add to

        ii. Revelation 22:19

        iii. Powerful in influence

        iv. Written for a purpose (2 Timothy 3:16; 1 John 5:13)

    c. Reveals eternal truth (Psalm 119:89; Matthew 24:35)

2. The right foundation stone: needs of the people

    a. General needs: needs of people in general

    b. Specific needs: individual needs

    c. Requires constant balance with the left foundation stone

3. The left pillar: helping people think

    a. Three stages of thinking

        i. Knowledge: intellectual, or academic; experiential; controlled

        ii. Spiritual understanding: the ability to act and think spiritually

        iii. Wisdom: putting Biblical understanding into action

4. The right pillar: helping people value

    a. Emotional aspects of Christian growth

    b. Maturity in Christian growth

        i. Openness

        ii. Willingness to share

        iii. Removing barriers

        iv. Balance

5. The center pillar: helping people relate

    a. Loving God

    b. Loving people

    c. Matthew 22:37–39

6. The capstone: growth

7. The circle: being surrounded by the Holy Spirit

Don't miss the importance of what William Yount has accomplished. In the first place, he puts educational psychology in a Christian perspective by showing the importance of having the Bible as the main foundation for all of learning. He further shows the importance of a Christian perspective by illustrating the ministry of the Holy Spirit in the life of every believer. Second, he illustrates four of the most basic educational principles, namely: (1) students have individual needs; (2) students need thinking skills; (3) students need to know how to relate to others; and (4) students need to learn what things are valuable and what things are not. In other words, students need to know how to set priorities. His final principle is illustrated by the fact that students are meant to grow. Growth is what all of education is about.

Look at the following chart to see the relationship between Yount's model and educational psychology.

The Disciplers' Model and Educational Psychology

Educational Element	Educational Content
The Bible	Mastery
Needs of learners	Individual differences
Thinking skills	cognitive domain
Values/Priorities	Affective domain
Relationships	Social/Group dynamics
Growth in the Lord	Maturation
Holy Spirit	Guide and Teacher

For Further Discussion

1. Explain how psychology is actually a way of thinking, a way of approaching education, and not just a curriculum.

2. Review the definitions of educational psychology and discuss how they are similar to Christian education.

3. Encourage someone to Google both the Old Deluder Satan Act of 1647 and the Sunday School Movement of 1780. (You may even want to include the New England Primer, and the Hornbook.)

4. Look at the picture of Yount's model.[2]

Discipler's Model

Used by permission of Dr. William R. Yount. Please see *Created To Learn* or visit his website http://drrickyount.com/disciplers-model/.

Notes

1. Yount, William R. *Created To Learn*. Nashville, TN: Broadman & Holman Publishers, 1996. 4.

2. Yount, William R. *Called to Reach: Equipping Cross-Cultural Disciplers,* Nashville, Tennessee: B&H Publishers, 2007.

Being Different is Good

10

We often acknowledge that people are different. We say it about children. We say it about adults. We say it about those from other cultures. We say it, but do we really believe it? We say that children are different, but then we expect them to act alike. As it relates to teaching and education, it is certainly true that students are different. Students with the same teacher, in the same classroom, with the same text and materials earn different grades. One of the biggest challenges for teachers is understanding what causes differences. Think back to your own experiences in school. You probably learned some concepts and subjects more easily than other subjects, and you may have learned some things more easily than other people. Or it's possible that learning was hard for you while it seemed easier for others. This aspect of learning is another reason why even Christian teachers in Sunday Schools, vacation Bible school (VBS), etc. need to have some knowledge of educational psychology.

Consider these questions as you think about the fact that people are different:

1. How do we learn?

2. What does it mean to "learn" something?

3. Why can we remember some things more easily than others?

4. Why do some people struggle in learning a subject while others seem to have no problem?

5. Why do some people intentionally fail a subject?

6. What does it mean to be "educated"?

7. Why is it that each member of a class with the same text, the same notes, the same teacher, and the same tests will more than likely have different results?

8. Why is it you can know something for a test, but forget it when the test is over?

9. Why is it that the item on a test you miss is the one you remember more?

These are just a few of the questions that deserve honest answers when it comes to being an effective teacher. Learning is a personal responsibility and involves a variety of factors. Perhaps another question needs to be asked as well. That question is: why worry about how we learn? Part of the answer is that learning occurs every day, is often unnoticed, and is based on how you think. However, when it comes to learning, teachers need to be aware of three fallacies concerning what teaching is all about. The first fallacy is this: *To teach is to tell.* This fallacy assumes that teaching is nothing more than verbalizing facts and that learning occurs when information is given to students. All you have to do to see the fallacy in this statement is to reflect back on your own school days. Many times you had teachers who gave you facts, but many of those facts never made it to your brain. That leads to the second fallacy: *To tell is to know.* This aspect assumes students will correctly understand. Again, your experiences of days gone by prove the fallacy of that statement. The third fallacy is: *To know is to do.* This assumes that students automatically change their conduct or behavior merely because a teacher has given them a set of facts and information. If you have been teaching for any period of time, you know this is a fallacy. You have no doubt presented some very good biblical truth to your students and yet, unfortunately, some of your students still have not changed or applied the truth to their behavior.

All of us understand that learning is an important part of life, yet we still struggle with what is involved in learning. Learning is often a mystery and no one can tell you with certainty how it really happens. Every teacher is aware that there are barriers to learning. Quite often students face obstacles and even limitations when it comes to learning. Some of the barriers to learning are related to the students as individuals. Many times students are faced with physical barriers such as body organs that don't work properly; the brain itself; sleep deprivation; nutritional deficiencies; or chemical imbalance. Sometimes the barriers are related to a psychological disorder such as stress; trauma; trouble with retention; avoidance of change; laziness and wrong priorities; or general apathy. Other barriers to learning may be something as simple as stumbling blocks from others such as peers and even cultural values. It's hard to believe, but there are still some cultures that shun education and even look down upon it. What faces the Christian in our culture is often related to differences of opinion between a Christian worldview and secularism.

In a small textbook like this one, space does not allow for a lengthy discussions regarding all that is involved in learning. However, it is important that you become aware of the different levels of learning. Two things are meant by "levels of learning." First, not everyone learns the same way, at the same speed, with the same retention. Part of this is because not every student has the same motivation or desire to learn. Secondly, the levels of learning involve at least four basic concepts of education. Each of these concepts is complex within themselves and, again, individuals respond to them differently. Educators refer to the concepts as the ABCDs of learning.

A: affective

Affective learning refers to the emotions and attitudes students bring with them to a classroom. It refers to the fact that some individuals like some things and dislike other things. When students come to a classroom, they have a variety of emotions and attitudes regarding things like the subject matter presented, the teacher, and even their peers. These emotions and attitudes may be positive or negative, but either way they affect the learning process. Educators should be aware that affective learning involves five additional levels: (1) *receiving:* is the student willing and open to learning? (2) *responding:* does a student display a sustained consideration for a particular viewpoint? (3) *valuing:* does a student have a preference or commitment to a particular viewpoint? (4) *organization:* does the student make any attempt to internalize his life to that particular viewpoint? (5) *characterization:* are the student's values beginning to be played out in life? Does what he believe become who and what he is?

It's obvious that each of these is related to Christianity as well.

B: behavioral

The behavioral level, or concept, of learning is related to physical skills and habits. Involved in this are preparation, practice, and performance. *Preparation* refers to the student's awareness of things around him that are learned through the senses as well as having a readiness or desire to learn. *Practice* is typically done under the guidance of someone else, such as a teacher or someone trained in a particular area. In other words, practice is much like a coach giving instructions to a team as to how a particular game needs to be played. *Performance* involves the student striving for excellence with a degree of confidence.

C: cognitive

Cognitive refers to the concepts of knowledge and intellectual skills. Learning new information, storing that information in the brain, and having the ability to recall that information at a later date are a small part of the cognitive domain of learning. Cognitive development quite often involves hearing new information that may conflict with what may have been previously known. In that case, cognitive development has to make adjustments. Teachers who have been trained in the field of education to become teachers are familiar with what is called Bloom's Taxonomy. B.S. Bloom classified learning into three types with each one having varying degrees of complexity. His three groups of learning are: (1) cognitive, or what we know; (2) affective, or how we feel; and (3) psychomotor, or the skills we have learned or achieved. Another aspect of cognitive learning refers to remembering and forgetting. It includes things like short-term and long-term memory and even memory decay, which refers to the fact that some things leave our conscious mind over a period of time. There are two educational reasons why this happens. First, inactivity, such as the adage that says, "use it or lose it," and, secondly, interference, which refers to previous knowledge interfering with new information.

D: dispositional

Dispositional learning refers to the values and tendencies that cause us to act. Each of us has an intellect, a will, and emotions, and each of these motivates us to action. Dispositions are related to the formation of habits. The goal of dispositional learning is to get us to do things by "second nature" or to do things automatically because they have become so entrenched in our minds. For instance, we seldom even have to stop and think about how to eat. We have learned that even in the dark we can take a fork, put food on it and put it in our mouth. Once you have learned to ride a bike, you never forget it. The goal of Christian education is for teachers to so inspire students that they will take that same approach with spiritual truth. Regularly acting or behaving in a spiritual way is what God wants of every believer.

Theories of learning in a secular sense are based on two educational foundations: psychological and educational. For the believer, there is a third foundation: the spiritual. It is our responsibility as Christian teachers to help our students learn they are not fully or truly educated without this third foundation. In summary, let me mention that learning itself involves five important elements. Those elements, hopefully, can be remembered by using the acrostic L.E.A.R.N.

L: levels of learning

What can we learn? God made us in His image. We are intellectual beings. We can create, invent, and build. All you need to do to verify this is to look at how far we have come in the field of technology and science. Most of the conveniences we now enjoy like electricity, computers, telephones, and the like are relatively young. Because we are made in His image, and because we have the possibility of having the mind of Christ, there is no limit to what the human mind can learn.

E: extent of learning

How well we learn in great measure depends upon us. Motivation, attitudes, and purpose are involved. The greater and higher the motivation, the greater the learning; but in another sense, as teachers we have the privilege and responsibility of inspiring students to greater heights. As believers we have the privilege and responsibility to do what we do, including learning, to His glory.

A: avenues of learning

Each of us learns in different ways. Some learn best by *linguistic intelligence*, which relates to using language effectively. The next time you sing a hymn or read a poem, think about the skills it took to create it. Most likely an individual with linguistic intelligence wrote these pieces. Some learn best by *logical-mathematical intelligence*. These individuals have the ability to reason and to use logic, and they are typically gifted in various areas of science. Some learn by *spatial intelligence*. They have the ability to recognize details, to imagine, to see things in their minds as if they were already reality. The next time you're in church, look at the design and style. Someone designed it and saw the finished product before the building was even started. Others learn best by *musical intelligence*. They have the ability to create, comprehend, and appreciate music. But musical intelligence is not limited to musicians. You may have learned the alphabet as a child by a little song. You may have learned the books of the Bible through a chorus you learned in Vacation Bible School or Sunday School. Still others learn through *bodily-kinesthetic intelligence*. These people are often some of the best athletes and other performers. Some learn best by *interpersonal intelligence*. They understand people. They have the ability to see things in people that others miss. Others learn by *intrapersonal intelligence*. They know themselves. They know their strengths and weaknesses. Others learn by *naturalist intelligence*. They see nature as more than plants and animals. They see patterns in all of life. Some even learn through a combination of all of these methods.

When you look at the variety of ways in which the human spirit learns, you cannot help but think of the gifts of the Holy Spirit. The gifts of the Holy Spirit are directly related to your own personal way of learning. Have you noticed that people who don't sing very well don't become music directors? Go back and read the accounts of spiritual gifts in Romans 12:3–8, 1 Corinthians 12:12–31, and Ephesians 4:11–16. We are different and this is good. The difference gives us an opportunity to be of service to each other. What you can't do someone else can and what they can't do you can. The wonder of it all is that with all our diversity and differences, we are still one in the body of Christ. We all need Christ and we need each other as well.

Further Discussion

1. What subject(s) in school did you find easy? Why?

2. What subject(s) in school did you find difficult? Why?

3. How did a teacher help you understand a subject that was hard for you?

4. Review the ABCDs of learning and show how they relate to Christian education.

5. Do you remember a test question you missed in your earlier days of school? Why do you think you still remember it?

6. Using the eight learning styles listed under the avenues of learning, let some of your students state which way they learn best and why.

LEARNING DIFFERENCES AND LEARNING NEEDS

11

Let's do a little review before we begin this chapter. Thus far, you have read about what is involved in the field of psychology (Chapter 8); what educational psychology is (Chapter 9); and that being different is good (Chapter 10). The underlying theme of these three chapters is to help you realize that an effective teacher seeks to have an understanding of students, understands good educational principles, and recognizes that students are truly different, if not even unique. This chapter continues with the concept that people are not only different physically, they differ intellectually. They differ intellectually in not only what and how much they know, but how they learn. Chapter 10 lists eight different styles of learning that illustrate those differences.

One of the problems in education today is the attitude of putting labels on students. We have labels like learning disabilities, autism, ADHD, OCD, and a host of others. The problem with putting labels on people is that not only is it unfair to them, too often it brings a prejudice in the mind of the teacher towards a particular student. You've heard the old adage, "don't judge a book by its cover," but unfortunately that's exactly what is often done when a student is labeled. Understand that students are different, but look at those differences as blessings, not as obstacles.

A label often used today to describe students (children, teens, and adults) is the term "disabled." It carries the idea that a student has an inability to do something specific. Another term is "handicapped." The original background of the term comes from the phrase "cap-in-hand" when people would have to beg to survive. It was then, and still is today, a demeaning term. In one sense, all of us have areas in which we are weak. Let me suggest a couple of ways to more effectively view those who may have special needs.

1. Speak directly to them, not about them.

2. Look them in the eye when talking to them.

3. Talk in a normal voice, unless you know they have hearing difficulties.

4. Practice disability etiquette. This can be done in a variety of ways. One of the best approaches is to simply use "person-first" language. Use words like, "they are people with learning disabilities" instead of

calling them disabled people. Say they are "receiving special education," not that they are special education people. Say they are "people with epilepsy," not that they are epileptics. In other words, refer to them as people first, and mention their special need second.

The fact that people are different and have different ways of learning is related to the whole concept of intelligence. What does it mean to be intelligent? Intelligence has three themes. First, it carries the idea that an individual has the capacity to learn. Secondly, it refers to the total knowledge a person my already have. Thirdly, it assumes an individual has the ability to adapt to new situations.

Intelligence is also understood by recognizing the different types of intelligence. Eight of these have already been presented in a previous chapter. Others types of intelligence include what is referred to as "g," or *general intelligence*. This is the kind of mental energy a person has to perform any mental task. *Fluid intelligence* refers to a person's mental efficiency and reasoning ability. Another form of intelligence is *crystallized intelligence,* which refers to a person's ability to use problem-solving methods that are appropriate within a cultural context. Others have an intelligence called *spiritual* and *existential,* which means they have the ability to contemplate the bigger questions about the meaning of life. Another type of intelligence is known as the *triarchic theory,* or successful intelligence. By its very name we can see that it involves three areas: (1) *analytical:* the mental process that leads to intelligent behavior; (2) *creativity:* which means that through insight (ability to deal with novel situations) and automaticity, a person begins to behave in an automatic way without even thinking; and (3) *practicality:* a person using the strength of his abilities to make decisions for careers, etc. Whatever the style of intelligence a person may have, it is a basic assumption in education that intelligence is a continual process.

In days gone by, the church almost ignored those with special needs. It's encouraging to see that situation change as time goes on. Regardless, today's Christian teachers in church settings need to be aware of some of the common characteristics of people with learning disabilities. Some of the common characteristics, but not all, include the following:

- Problems in one or more academic area

- Poor coordination

- Problems paying attention

- Organizing, interpreting visual and/or auditory information

• Problems in thinking skills, memory, and speech

• Problems in keeping friends

More specific disabilities that in all honesty may be open to controversy need to be mentioned as well. The severity and even validity of some of these disabilities are still being evaluated by educators and psychologists, but the truth is that the following disabilities are a part of our culture and society. Time and space does not permit lengthy information, but an effective teacher should at least be aware of these disabilities.

• Hyperactivity and Attention Disorders

These typically involve two kinds of problems: those with attention disorders and those with what is called impulsive-hyperactivity problems.

• Attention-deficit hyperactivity problems (ADHD)

This includes areas such as disruptive behavior disorders, over-activity, and excessive difficulty in paying attention.

• Language/Communication Disorders

This includes the more severe types of disorders such as speech disorder with the inability to produce speech sounds effectively. It includes those with voicing problems, which refers to an inappropriate pitch, quality, loudness, or intonation of the voice. It may also include the inability to express oneself like those of their own age.

• Emotional/Behavioral Difficulties

In many ways, these comprise a larger part of the population and include a variety of areas. This term refers to a type of behavior that deviates from the norm. Some of the possible types would include: (1) disruptive behavior, such as ADHD and ODD, which is an oppositional defiant disorder exemplified by breaking rules, fighting, bullying, and being cruel to others; (2) eating disorders, which includes both anorexia nervosa and bulimia nervosa; (3) mood disorders, which are called affective disorders, such as depression, bipolar, manic depression, and mood swings; (4) tic disorders, which are involuntary movements of muscle groups; and (5) addictive tendencies.

• Health impairment

The issues of personal health comprise another large segment of the population. Unfortunately, churches are experiencing this as well. In some cases, people who would normally be faithful to church no longer attend because of personal health issues. Among the health issues are: (1) cerebral palsy (physical coordination difficulty); (2) spasticity, or tight, tense muscles; (3) seizure disorder, such as epilepsy; (4) asthma; and (5) diabetes.

- Miscellaneous Issues

People experience a variety of other issues as well. They include things like: (1) vision problems, such as low vision, or the need to have objects close to the eyes; (2) hearing difficulty; (3) and autism and Asperger syndrome, which involves a lack of verbal and non-verbal communication skills and social interaction.

In addition to the problems listed here, there is another group of people who have unusual and specific needs that the church seldom even thinks about. That group consists of those who are classified as gifted. You might not think that these individuals have problems, but often when it comes to education and knowledge, they become bored because they are not challenged enough. Take this group into consideration when planning your lessons each week.

Why even mention all of these areas? The simple truth is, people who have these difficulties are still people and in need of spiritual truth. You can't read the New Testament without seeing that Jesus was concerned about all kinds of people with all kinds of situations. In recent years, churches have improved by installing ramps for those confined to wheelchairs as well as making arrangements for other handicap needs, but don't forget those who have emotional, psychological, social, and educational needs as well. It is to be admitted that meeting these kinds of needs takes individuals who have a heart for people. It takes training to deal with many of these issues, but just because people have special needs, there is no reason for Christian educators to avoid these students.

People with needs, even in church settings, range from those who are severely mentally challenged to those who are extremely intelligent. How can such a broad range be ministered to effectively? An even greater concern is the fact that the range of differences involves all age levels. That is, children, adolescents, and adults comprise these differences and what works with one age may not be appropriate for another age. The church faces a problem that secular institutions do not face. Secular institutions often administer tests to people to determine their intellectual ability and based on the results of that testing, individuals are placed in an appropriate class or grade level. The church does not have that privilege. In fact, in their book, *Introduction To Psychology and Counseling: Christian Perspectives and Applications*, the authors state: "Giving IQ tests is not appropriate for Sunday schools. While school grades may be predicted from IQ scores, there is no evidence that performance in Sunday school is correlated with IQ."[1] The authors, however, are very quick to point out that other matters beyond IQ are more important. Other matters like ethics, morality, and an individual's relationship with Christ are certainly more important. They further state:

> "Christians should also be aware of the danger of pride. Frequently, individuals with high IQs tend to be prideful. Intelligence is a complex entity, and intellectual ability is undoubtedly influenced by both inherited traits and environmental influences. Although some persons are born with a greater intellectual capacity than others, early childhood stimulation and opportunities for cultural development (schools, modeling, and verbal interaction) can also influence the development of measurable intellectual capacity. Christians who have a high IQ should avoid pride and humbly acknowledge a greater responsibility to use their intelligence to God's glory. Christians with an average IQ should not feel second-class or cheated, but should take advantage of all available alternatives to utilize their abilities to God's glory. God recognizes no difference between rich or poor, smart or mentally handicapped, since all Christians are his children through faith in Jesus Christ (Galatians 3:26–29)." [2]

For Further Discussion

1. Discuss the concept of the original meaning of "handicap."

2. Review the different types of intelligence and give an opportunity for class members to express their preferences.

3. Consider tactfully asking class members about possible family situations caused by the range of differences in their family regarding the mentally challenged and giftedness.

4. Conduct a general discussion as to how your class may give assistance to those in your church family and/or community who care for those with special needs.

5. Survey your church property to see if there are things that need to be done to make your church accessible to those with special needs and then devise a plan to meet those needs.

Notes

1. Meier, Paul D., et al. *Introduction to Psychology and Counseling.* Grand Rapids, MI: Baker, 2004. 150.

2. Meier, Paul D., et al. *Introduction to Psychology and Counseling.* Grand Rapids, MI: Baker, 2004. 154.

LEARNING PLANS

12

You've heard the old adage, "I saved the best 'til last." I hope that's true about this chapter. It's now time to deal with where the rubber meets the road.

Effective teachers know what it is they want to teach. They not only know what they're going to teach, they plan to get there. Professional teachers call these lesson plans. A better term is "learning plans" because effective teachers plan for their students to learn. Unfortunately, and too often, teachers shy away from this concept of teaching, but the idea is a valid one. Stop and think about it. Other professions have plans. A football or basketball coach has a game plan. He has scouted out the opposing team. He learns everything he can about the offense and defense of his opponent. He knows which player needs to be guarded. An airline pilot has a flight plan. In fact, it's mandatory. He has to file the flight plan before he is permitted to take off. An architect has a full set of plans with every detail imaginable. Even in surgery, a doctor plans out his strategy.

What about the field of politics? You can be sure that a politician maps out a strategy for his campaign. He knows which areas of the country are more crucial for votes than others. He knows which issues to stress and which issues are least important. A business executive has a plan. He knows his competition. He knows the market. If you go on a diet, it's been proven that the best way to lose weight is to have a plan. Coaches, pilots, architects, politicians, business executives, dieters, and a host of other individuals plan their work in advance. Their success depends on it.

Teaching should be no different, particularly when it comes to Christian education. The day is long gone, or should be, when teachers believe all they have to do is stand before a class and expect the Lord to fill their mouths with what to say. Please don't take offense to that statement. I do believe a teacher of Christian truth should rely on the spiritual anointing of the Holy Spirit, but I firmly believe it is the responsibility of teachers to do whatever is necessary to be well prepared so the Holy Spirit can fill them with His power and anointing. Paul says it like this: "Do your best to present yourself to God as one approved, a worker who does not need to be ashamed and who correctly handles the word of truth" (2 Timothy 2:15, NIV).

To understand the importance of developing learning plans, let me first explain why such a concept is valid and even essential.

1. *Planning influences what students will learn.* Maybe the reason some students haven't learned spiritual truth significantly is because teachers have not been sure what it was they were going to teach. When you have a plan, you know what you're going to teach.

2. *Planning reduces uncertainty in teaching.* When you're not sure and confident about what is going to be taught, teaching can be stressful. Knowing what you're going to teach builds confidence and enthusiasm.

3. *Learning plans are different from curriculum guides.* Curriculum guides are beneficial, but usually the publisher of the curriculum provides them. They are helpful and should be used to give a teacher important background information and other resources, but a curriculum guide does not know the individuals who will be in the classroom. Teachers are the only ones who know that.

4. *Plans can be tailored to your students and yourself.* Learning plans are related to the personality of the teacher. What works for one teacher may not work for another one. What works in one setting may not work in another setting.

5. *The best of learning plans will allow you to be flexible.* Having a useable plan makes it easier to be flexible. Unforeseen circumstances will arise that you had not planned on, but at least when you know what you are hoping to do, you can be better prepared to make adjustments.

The styles of learning plans are as varied as the teachers. For an illustration, take any of the letters of the Apostle Paul and use this simple outline: the *author*, the *audience*, the *analysis,* and the *application.* Write those four words down on a sheet of paper and put the appropriate information under each word. Under the word "author" write the Apostle Paul. (Obviously if it's a different author, you would write that name down.) Then write down any other pertinent information you want your class to know about the author, such as who he is, where he was, etc. Under the word audience, write down to whom the letter is written. Is the letter written to an individual or to a group, such as a church? Under the word analysis, write down why the letter is written. You may have to read a little further to find this out, but if you don't know why something is written, you'll have difficulty explaining the letter. Under the word application, write down what it is you hope your students will glean from this. Look at the outline again in this way: the author (who wrote it?); the audience (to whom is it written?); the analysis (why was the passage written?); and the application (what do you want your students to learn?). Believe me, writing down something as simple as this makes your teaching more enjoyable to you and easier to understand for your students. Using these four words is a way of giving your students a "hook" on which they can hang information.

Another style of writing a learning plan is to write down a variety of objectives. What is it you're hoping to get across to your students? A variety of objectives can be written, but two of the simplest types are instructional (sometimes called cognitive objectives) and behavioral. Instructional objectives are clear, well thought out statements of what you hope your students will learn or know. Behavioral objectives are a little harder to write because you have to be able to actually observe a change, or test what students know that they didn't know before. Take for an illustration the first letter of Paul to a young man by the name of Timothy. Your learning plan would look something like this:

The First Letter of Paul to Timothy

- The Author: the Apostle Paul

- The Audience: the young man, Timothy

- The Analysis:

    o Paul is writing Timothy to encourage him to be a faithful minister of the Gospel.

    o Paul is writing Timothy to encourage him not to be intimidated by other older believers.

    o Paul is writing Timothy to express his appreciation and love for him.

    o Instructional objectives:

        ■ I want my students to know who the author of the book of 1 Timothy is.

        ■ I want my students to know why Paul is writing to Timothy.

        ■ I want my students to know something about who Timothy is, such as:

            • Who were his parents?

            • Where was Timothy serving as a pastor?

        ■ I want my students to know how Paul encouraged Timothy.

    o Behavioral objectives:

        ■ My students will be able to state who wrote this letter.

        ■ My students will be able to discuss what kind of person

Timothy was.

> ▪ My students will be able to answer the following questions:
>
>   • Who was Timothy's mother?
>
>   • Who was Timothy's grandmother?
>
>   • Where was Timothy serving as a pastor?

• The Application:

  o This may be accomplished by allowing students to tell you what it's like to be a young person in today's world and how a young man like Timothy can be an inspiration to them. This is an opportunity for you to ask your students what such a letter means to them, or more important, how they would respond if they were to receive such a letter.

In the field of education there are three areas of objectives, which are called domains. Those three domains are: (1) cognitive; (2) affective; and (3) psychomotor. The cognitive domain refers to the thinking process of a student. When teaching to the cognitive domain, you will want to help students not only know something they might not have known before, but be sure they comprehend it as well. The affective domain refers to how students feel, or how they respond to what is being taught. The psychomotor domain refers to the behavioral aspect, or the differences seen in a student's actions in light of what he or she has learned.

Basically, a learning plan involves the writing down of what it is you want your students to know and learn. This is accomplished by using instructional objectives, or cognitive learning, and behavioral objectives, or how it is you're hoping your students will behave. In addition to the objectives of a learning plan are two other ingredients. They are the methods and the materials you will utilize. Again, you actually write down on paper the method or methods you will be using to teach a given lesson. Your methods could include giving a lecture, using a question/answer technique, using a resource such as a video on the life of the Apostle Paul, or whatever method you choose. Write down the actual materials you will be using, such as a prepared outline for students to read so they can follow along with you, or a video and/or DVD.

To give you a handle on this concept, consider again Paul's letter to Timothy. Here is what a completed learning plan would look like:

Paul's First Letter To Timothy

- **Instructional (Cognitive) Objectives**
  - o I want my students to know the *author* of this letter.
  - o I want my students to know the *audience* of this letter.
  - o I want my students know the *analysis* of this letter.
  - o I want my students to know how the life of Timothy can be an encouragement to them.

- **Behavioral Objectives**
  - o My students will be able to say who wrote the letter of First Timothy.
  - o My students will be able to discuss what kind of person Timothy was.
  - o My students will be able to answer the following questions:
    - ■ Who was Timothy's mother?
    - ■ Who was Timothy's grandmother?
    - ■ Where was Timothy serving as a pastor?

- **Methods to be used**
  - o I will use a three-in-one approach including a PowerPoint presentation to show the points of the lesson as they are discussed.
  - o I will use a question/answer technique throughout the lesson to be sure the students know the characters in the letter to Timothy.

- **Materials Needed**
  - o Each student will be provided with an outline of the discussion.
  - o Equipment will be available for the PowerPoint presentation.
  - o Necessary pencils will be available, if needed.

When you look at this learning plan you may think, "That's a lot of work and effort." You're exactly right! Who has that kind of time? You do, when you think what you're doing is important. You do, when you see excellence as the goal of all teaching. You do, when you believe God deserves the best you can give Him. But look at the benefits of such a plan:

1. You will be better prepared to teach and being prepared makes the experience more personally enjoyable.

2. Being better prepared demonstrates to your students that they're worth it.

3. Being better prepared proves to your students that you enjoy what you're doing.

4. Having such a plan makes it easier for a substitute teacher to step into your place should that become necessary. (When you know you will be absent, inform someone that a learning plan is available for a substitute teacher.)

5. Being better prepared demonstrates to your students that learning biblical truth is important. In fact, two guiding truths should motivate both you and your class. They are:

• "But in your hearts set apart Christ as Lord. Always be prepared to give an answer to everyone who asks you to give the reason for the hope that you have" (1 Peter 3:15, NIV).

• "But grow in the grace and knowledge of our Lord and Savior Jesus Christ..." (2 Peter 3:18, NIV).

For Further Discussion

1. Discuss the importance of having a plan as it relates to the careers of a coach, an architect, a doctor, a pilot, and a politician.

2. Discuss the benefits of a teacher creating a learning plan.

3. Be sure you understand the difference in a curriculum guide and a learning plan.

4. Select one of your favorite Bible passages and make a learning plan for it as if you were going to teach it next Sunday.

5. Discuss the differences between instructional objectives and behavioral objectives.

EPILOGUE

Every teacher needs to be F.A.T. Don't be offended by that. It's not what you think. Those three letters stand for three more traits of effective teachers: *faithful, approachable,* and *teachable.* These traits actually undergird everything that makes an effective teacher. Whether you realized it or not, your best teachers, and the ones you still remember, exhibited these three traits and these traits motivated them to do everything else they did to make you enjoy your educational experience.

Teachers are often considered good, or effective, based on the learning level of the students. However, in recent days, it has been discussed that it's not a fair criteria for evaluating a teacher. More educators and psychologists are discovering that one teacher may be effective for one student and not effective for another. It used to be a common statement that if a student did not learn it was because the teacher had not taught. That has been revised as well because the simple truth is, students have a responsibility in the learning process too. It's not always a teacher's fault when the student has not learned. But the question still remains: what is effective teaching and what is an effective teacher?

Chapter 9 exposed you to educational psychology. Such a discipline involves not only knowing the subject matter, but knowing how to control a classroom, make learning plans, manage your time, and a host of other skills. Over and over the college student who prepares to be a teacher is reminded of the characteristics of effective teachers. Educational psychology, among other things, states there are three qualities of teachers that are important: clarity and organization, warmth, and knowledge.

Clarity and organization

This may seem to be very insignificant, but how you speak and how you organize your thoughts and materials is important. One of the greatest gifts of teaching is a good voice. In actuality, your voice is an instrument. It has the capability of being loud or soft and other volumes in between. The voice may be used as a means of discipline or of getting someone's attention. The voice may be easy to listen to or monotone. As a teacher, you need to know your own strengths and weaknesses. Record yourself or ask someone to evaluate your voice to see what you might want to do to improve.

What about your organizational skills? Is your presentation in a logical, sequential order or are you prone to rambling? In most cases, when you prepare to teach a lesson, you may be supplied with materials such as a teacher's manual, which gives you the information in an already-organized format. Following that structure is helpful, but the best method is to organize the material in a way that fits your personality. If need be, change the wording from the manual to fit your personality. Seasoned teachers will tell you that lessons of your own making are the easiest lessons to teach.

Warmth

Another word for warmth is "approachable." Elsewhere in this book it is pointed out that teachers should be approachable. Warmth carries the idea of having concern or care. Warmth is the idea that teachers are aware that students are not just part of a class. Students have a life outside of class. They are part of a family. They may be students in an elementary, high school, or college setting. They may have a job. They may be without a much-needed job. They may have family problems. A teacher who characterizes warmth recognizes all of these factors and more.

Knowledge

An effective teacher knows the subject matter they teach. That does not mean they know it all, but it does mean that what they don't know, they are continually seeking to learn.

Knowledge of the subject

More than likely those reading this are teachers of Christian education classes and/or Bible curriculum. Obviously, it's imperative for you to know the subject. In a practical sense, it means that an effective Bible teacher has a workable knowledge of the Bible. It means that you know some of the basic language associated with the Bible. Certainly an effective teacher needs to know such terms as inspiration, revelation, inerrancy, and infallible. An effective Bible teacher should know some of the history of the Bible, such as who the authors are, in what language the Bible was first written, how many divisions of the Bible exist, and how many individual books are in the Bible. All of these are elementary topics, but they need to be part of the teacher's knowledge base in order for him or her to understand some of the more advanced teachings of the Bible.

Knowledge of the students

What age do you teach? What do you know about them? An effective teacher has knowledge of the characteristics of their students. You may recall that earlier in this book it was pointed out that Jesus was discerning of His students. He knew something about them as individuals. He knew something about them as being part of a group. An effective teacher is aware that students are affected by many emotional, social, physical, psychological, and spiritual factors. Knowing each of these traits and how your students develop in each of these areas will enhance your teaching ministry.

Knowledge of techniques

There are two important educational principles to be mentioned here. First, in one sense, all students learn in a similar fashion. That is, all students have to be exposed to things they do not know. Secondly, students learn individually. One student may learn one way while another student may learn in a completely different way. The effective teacher is continually seeking to understand which way is best to teach his or her students.

Organization

In addition to having the characteristics of clarity and organization, warmth, and knowledge, effective teachers are planners. You have heard the expression, "plan your work and work your plan." That's a good motto for every teacher. Planning is the first step in the specifics of teaching. It influences not only *how* students will learn, but also *what* they will learn. It reduces uncertainty in teaching. It involves a variety of levels.

Organization by the year

Don't let this overwhelm you. Knowing what a particular curriculum will be for an entire year provides an opportunity to get a bird's-eye view of what's coming. It gives you an opportunity to begin looking for ways to make your presentations effective. You may find that some parts of the curriculum are of less interest to you than others, and knowing this ahead of time gives you the opportunity to ask someone to team-teach with you. Perhaps you have an interest and expertise in one area while someone else has a greater interest and expertise in another area. Between the two of you, an excellent presentation can be achieved.

Organization by the term or the unit

Typically, Sunday School classes are divided into four quarters. Each quarter is a term. Look at the curriculum for the given term. Read the material for the entire quarter and get a bird's-eye view of what's coming. Knowing in advance allows your mind to begin thinking about what you would like to do and the most appropriate way to do it.

Organizatation by the week

During the week is where the final planning gets serious. What are you going to do with the lesson at hand? Teachers in both public and private schools are very familiar with lesson plans. They are required to have them and even required to let their supervisor see them. This is not to advocate that Christian educators should do this, but we should be just as prepared for our classes in spiritual truth as other teachers are with secular knowledge.

A teacher's lesson plan often involves four elements: objectives, materials, methods, and evaluation. The objectives often include cognitive objectives, or things you want your students to <u>know</u>, behavioral objectives, or how you want your students to <u>respond to and act on</u>, and affective objectives, or how you want you students to <u>feel</u> as a result of the lesson. The objectives are usually written in the form of a sentence, but you may want to shorten them to just a few words.

Writing out such a plan with these objectives assures that you will be prepared for the lesson. Your plan can be as simple or as lengthy as you prefer. Even if you don't take the actual time to write out the plan, having it in your mind will make your teaching far more effective. Taking the time to plan your lesson in this detail will give you more confidence and assurance that you are ready. It boils down to this: Your cognitive objectives tell you what you want your students to know. Your behavior objectives tell you how you want your students to act or respond. Your affective objectives tell you how your students will feel. The materials and methods objectives will verify what you will need to teach the lesson.

Another aspect of learning plans is evaluation. Evaluation is not typically done in a Sunday School setting, and I'm not advocating that it should be, but the concept should be taken seriously. Evaluation refers to finding out how well you as the teacher are doing, or have done, and how much your students have actually learned. Whether you write out your evaluation or not, you need to be aware that there are two types of evaluations that will let you know if you accomplished all of your objectives. First, there are student evaluations. These may take the form of an actual test, projects, reports, or something as simple as getting their response as to how well you are doing. If you ask them their opinion, be prepared. Some students can be very brutally honest, but that's what you want. You want to know how you're doing. You want to know the areas that need to be improved. You want to know if you're getting through to them. The second type of evaluation is one that you do for yourself. In other words, take a self-evaluation. How well do <u>you</u> think you did? Do you feel you did what you planned? If not, why not? Guard against putting yourself down too much, but at the same time recognize your own strengths and weaknesses.

Effective teachers are good planners. They know their subject matter. They know something about the characteristics of the students they teach. They know about the best methods of teaching. They know that not all students learn the same way. They know that what works for one teacher may not work for another teacher. You need to determine what works best for you. And while it is important to be a good planner and to even consider actually writing out a learning plan, you need to understand that no one plan works for everyone. Your personality, your talent, and your students are what you need to consider.

Being a teacher is not for everyone. In fact, the Bible states it this way: "My brethren, be not many masters, knowing that we shall receive the greater condemnation" (James 3:1). The word James uses for teachers and or teaching is "masters." He is quick to point out that teachers have a tremendous responsibility because they are under constant scrutiny or evaluation and will actually be held accountable for what they teach. When a teacher intentionally fails to teach a truth, they are held accountable, but when they intentionally teach something that is not true they will be judged as well.

In summary, a teacher has three relationships: (1) a personal relationship with Christ which involves salvation; (2) a public relationship to their church, which involves service; and (3) a preparation relationship which involves their personal study. All three relationships interact with each other and assist in the process of being an effective teacher.

THREE THAT MATTERED

Are teachers really important? What kind of influence do they have on their students? What kind of impact do they leave on a society? These questions have been asked probably as long as there have been teachers and students. Part of the answer to these questions is in your own experience. All you have to do is think back over your school days. It's possible that even right now you are remembering a teacher who had a large affect on you. It could have been in kindergarten, elementary, high school or college. Hopefully, it was in all those areas. History gives us ample illustrations of the difference teachers make. Three such people are John Amos Comenius, Robert Raikes, and Johann Pestalozzi. You may not have heard of any of them, but their influence as educators still lives on. Who were they? Why are they so important? What can you and I as teachers learn from them?

John Amos Comenius (1592-1670)

You may have never heard the word "pansophy" but I guarantee you have been exposed to it. It simply means "universal knowledge." The idea of universal knowledge is seen in such curriculums as world literature, religions of the world, ancient history, world history, and a host of other related topics. Even more recent topics, such as new age ideas, are an attempt to expose people to a variety of different world views—so in that sense new age ideas are really not new at all. John Amos Comenius believed that pansophy was an important part of a person's education. In one sense, his view may be better understood by what we call being well-rounded. Comenius, unfortunately, did not have the advantage of being raised for very long by his parents. By the time he had reached age 12, both of his parents and two sisters had already died. He lived with relatives and did not have the opportunity to receive a good education. However, other events in his life provided him with an education that led to his becoming a priest of the Bohemian Brethren. Again, misfortune was his lot when his first wife and two children died. During the days of his priesthood, he wrote and published materials in Latin. In 1663 one of his publications, *The Gate of Tongues Unlocked and Opened*, was published in English. It was not a book about the theology of speaking in tongues, but rather a book about how to learn a language. Later in his life he wrote what has come to be known as one of his greatest works. While it was written in Latin it was later published in English under the title of *Comenius's visible world, or a nomenclature, and pictures, of all the chief things that are in the world*. The significance of this publication is in the fact that it became "...the first school book consistently to use pictures of things in the learning of language." It was the educational principle of Comenius that "...words must go with things and cannot properly be learned apart from them." Because of this publication, he has become known as the father of visual learning. Again, please note this was before there was any form of public education. A further insight into Comenius's educational ideas is seen in his view of what he called the threefold revelation that was set before mankind. That threefold revelation is: (1) the visible creation in which the power of God becomes evident; (2) mankind was created in the image of God and displays the wisdom of God as proof of God's existence; and (3) the scriptures as the Word of God. Comenius stated: "All that man needs to know and not know must be learned from the divine books: nature, the mind or spirit of man, and the Scriptures. For the achievement of this education, man has been supplied with his senses, his reason, and faith." It was the educational philosophy of Comenius that education should be provided for all ages of mankind. Further, he believed and taught that life is a school and a preparation for eternal life. A debate that is prevalent in educational circles of today was present even in his day. That debate being if a student fails, whose fault is it? Comenius believed that a student's failure was not his fault but "evidence of the teacher's inadequacy to perform his role as the servant of nature...as the obstetrician of knowledge." He has gone down in history as a pioneer in at least two areas of education: (1) the use of visuals as a means of enhancing learning; and (2) the importance of pedagogy, or methods of teaching, that fit the needs and learning levels of the student.

Robert Raikes (1736-1811)

The educational influence of Robert Raikes has influenced both secular and Christian education. Raikes is usually affiliated with Christian education, or at least religious education more than secular, but his influence in the public arena is well documented. Historians differ as to Raikes' being the originator of Sunday School, but they all agree he is the one who brought it to the forefront. However, you must understand that Sunday School in Raikes' day is not what you and I are familiar with. We have the advantage of having good facilities, choices of curriculums, supportive parents, and in most cases, clean and well-groomed children. That was not the case in his day. Let's go back to the beginning.

Raikes himself was the son of a rather well-to-do business man who owned a newspaper in Gloucester, England. The newspaper was *Gloucester Journal*. Both father and son shared the same name of Robert. The father became known as Robert Raikes the Elder and the son became known as Robert Raikes the Younger. Robert the Elder owned the newspaper several years before the birth of Robert the Younger. When Robert the Elder died in 1757, Robert the Younger inherited the newspaper. By this time Robert the Younger had married and became the father of ten children: three sons and seven daughters. Raikes the Younger was also the grandson of an Anglican vicar named Timothy Raikes. Prior to Raikes' interest in children, particularly those who seemed to be disadvantaged and poor, Raikes was concerned about the social conditions of his community, especially the boys. Fathers, and often even some of the boys, worked six days a week in the factories and had little opportunity for any type of moral, religious, or educational improvement. Many of the men working in the factories were illiterate and on Sundays they seldom, if ever, attended church. In fact, quite frequently fathers would end up in jail because they were too poor to provide for their families.

Raikes would regularly visit the jails in an attempt to rehabilitate the men. The conditions of the jail were less than adequate and in many cases not even humane. Some of the inmates would go without food and others would have to beg from other prisoners for food. There were those in the community of Gloucester who could afford to send their children to schools that charged a small fee but most of the community could not. A few churches did try to reach out to the lower class and poor but not to large scale success. Raikes was moved by what he saw. Poor conditions in jail for adults, children roaming the streets on Sunday, and very little being done to change the situation. Raikes went to a preacher by the name of Thomas Stock of Ashbury, Berkshire, and asked him what he thought about a school on Sunday to try and reach some of the poor boys, and possibly adults as well. It was Raikes' intent to use the Bible as the textbook but then he realized that the boys he would be reaching could not read so a reading class would have to be included. Preacher Stock agreed and in July of 1780 Robert Raikes found a woman by the name of Mrs. Meredith who agreed to open her home to any children who wanted to come on Sunday for a class. Raikes himself made out a schedule and published it so it would be known what was happening:

"The children were to come after ten in the morning, and stay till twelve; they were then to go home and return at one; and after reading a lesson, they were to be conducted to Church. After Church, they were to be employed in repeating the catechism till after five, and then dismissed with an injunction to go home without making a noise."

When you add the hours up, it totals six hours. Quite different from your class today! The first few Sundays, very few children came. When Raikes asked some of the children who did come why others didn't come, they responded: "Cause our clothes ain't no good." Raikes began to change that by having clothes on hand but told the children who did come to tell others the only thing they needed was a clean face and combed hair. Soon more children began to come, including girls. It wasn't long before 100 children, ages six to fourteen, were coming to the schools that met on Sunday. Within two years other schools began to open in and around Gloucester. On November 3, 1783, Raikes published an article about the school and word began to spread. In 1784 two other publications, *Gentleman's Magazine*, and *Arminian Magazine*, a publication affiliated with the Methodist Preacher, John Wesley, wrote of the success in Gloucester. By 1784 it was believed there were 1,800 pupils in other areas of England. Some schools were even being attended by adults. By 1831, Sunday Schools in Great Britain were teaching 1,250,000 weekly, which was approximately 25 percent of the population. These Sunday Schools were in existence before state funding schools for the general public, and are said to be the forerunners of the current English school system.

As to be expected, not everyone was pleased with Raikes' idea. Some thought it was shameful to have such activity on a Sunday. Others thought the idea would take away the incentive for parents to teach their own children at home. Others even thought it was wrong for people to be employed, like Mrs. Meredith, to work on Sunday. Raikes himself was often ridiculed and called "Wild Bobby Goose" and his students were often called "Bobby Goose Rag-a-muffins." Fortunately, others began to see the importance of Raikes' idea, including Queen Charlotte, wife of George lll. She granted him an audience and encouraged others to follow his example. After Raikes' article in November of 1783, a movement in 1785 that became known as the Sunday School Society was established to coordinate and develop other schools. Those in the evangelical community, namely Hannah and Martha Moore, began to establish other schools and included the ideas of having good teaching methods (pedagogy) and other activities such as singing, seeking to meet the educational levels of the students. Until his death, Raikes continued to be involved with community concerns. He was instrumental in establishing an infirmary and a new and improved prison in his hometown of Gloucester. However, his greatest fame is the establishment of Sunday Schools that would bring about social changes in society over the next quarter of a century.

Johann Heinrich Pestalozzi (1746-1827)

Like Raikes, Pestalozzi was concerned for the improvement of the community in which he lived. He was born and lived in Zurich, Switzerland, and for a while sought to bring about social reform through politics. But after the death of a friend, he began to devote himself to education. At the age of 23 he married, and he and his wife tried their hand at farming. But because of a lack of business sense, the farm was a failure. He and his wife even tried to open a school in their farmhouse, but it failed as well. His desire to be an educator drove him to write about his philosophy and he was successful in publishing a book titled *The Evening Hours of A Hermit* (1780), which included some of his adages and other wise sayings as well as personal reflections. Following this book he published a more popular one titled *Leonard and Gertrude* (1781), a book that in his opinion showed the need for reformation in the personal life of an individual, a family, and consequently an entire community. The need for this reformation was illustrated in the efforts of a devoted woman. His most famous publication was titled *How Gertrude Teaches Her Children* (1801). It is thought that the character of Gertrude is a reference to the devoted woman referred to in his book of 1781. With Gertrude as the character, Pestalozzi describes some of the methods of teaching he felt were necessary for an effective teacher. Those methods included *observation,* or beginning with what a child already knows; *consciousness,* or an understanding of cognitive development; *speech,* or the importance of proper language and grammar; *measuring and numbers,* or math; *drawing,* or art appreciation; and *reckoning,* or thinking skills. It's interesting to note these areas comprise most of what children are exposed to in elementary grades and all of this was before the advent of what we now know as public education. Pestalozzi's philosophy further included pedagogy such as focusing in on the needs of a child's individual differences, the use of the senses in learning, and the personal activity of each student. Other areas of his educational psychology included general, moral, and intellectual education that was based on good human autonomy, or the need to teach children to be independent. In summary, Pestalozzi's philosophy was based on four themes: (1) home and family; (2) vocational and individual self-determination; and (3) state and nation. These three spheres stressed the importance of the family, the need for independence, and the fact that all individuals are a part of a social climate as well. The fourth sphere was related to the idea that a good education, after providing a means of personal satisfaction, would result in an inner peace and a strong belief in God. Prior to his death, Pestalozzi let it be known that in his opinion the greatest work he could ever accomplish would be his principles of education such as the development of observation as a tool for learning, the training of the whole person, and his compassion and concern for students. It has been said of him that he has had the deepest effect on all branches of education and his influence is far from being exhausted.

Lessons To Be Learned From These Three Men

Rather than trying to state any lengthy commentary about these men, since in so many ways they have similar characteristics, let me simply number what can be learned from them with just a few words of explanation.

1. **Each of them was committed to a faith in Christ.** This should dispel the criticism that is often hurled by the humanists and atheists of today who like to say that people of faith, both in the past and the present, are men of little intellectual ability. It is said of Comenius that he was even asked to become the President of the now famous Harvard University. What these three men accomplished, presented, and practiced is still a large part of all education procedures today. In fact, one is made to wonder if each of these three men in their own unique way are not the reason public education even came into existence.

2. **Each of them, in their own way, showed concern for what is known in the field of learning as holistic education.** They each believed students had educational, social, moral, and spiritual needs.

3. **Each of them stood for what they believed in even in the face of adverse circumstances.**

4. **Each of them used sound educational principles as a means of teaching that are still being used in all levels of classrooms today.**

5. **In many ways each of them was ahead of his time.** They stand as an illustration of the words of Solomon in Ecclesiastes 1:9: "...and there is no new thing under the sun."

6. **Each of them in their practice and belief lived by the adage all truth is God's truth.**

Each of the points listed above is an illustration of what real effective teaching, and teachers, are all about. They also illustrate that teachers never really know how far-reaching their influence may go. Only eternity itself reveals the influence of teachers.

For Further Discussion

1. Discuss with your students the similarities of Comenius, Raikes, and Pestalozzi.

2. What are some of the educational practices of today that were in existence during the days of Comenius, Raikes, and Pestalozzi?

3. Encourage three of your students to do further research on these three men. Let the three students choose the man they would like to research. (The use of Google.com is an excellent and easy resource.)

4. After reading about these three men, and perhaps even hearing from the three students who have agreed to do more research, what are some other lessons today's teachers can learn from them?

Bibliography and Other Resources

The following resources have been helpful in the writing of this chapter. You are also encouraged to go to Google.com and type in the individual names of these three men. There you will find much more information about each of them.

John Amos Comenius
• The Comenius Medal, a UNESCO award honoring outstanding achievements in the fields of education research and innovation, commemorates Comenius (Drucker, Peter; Transaction Publishers)

• Comenius' biography (www.apuritansmind.com/ChristianWalk/ McMahonComenius.htm)

• J.A. Comenius Museum in Uhersky Brod, Czech Republic

• Comenius Museum & Mausolem, Naarden, Netherlands

• The Visible World In Pictures (Orbis Pictus); online (www. gutenberg.org/ebooks/28299)

Robert Raikes
• Cunningham, Hugh. *Leisure in the Industrial Revolution.* London: Croom Helm, 1980.

• Dick, Malcolm. *The Myth of the Working Class Sunday School.* New York: Taylor and Francis, 1980.

• Kelly, Thomas. *A History of Adult Education in Great Britain.* Liverpool: Liverpool University Press, 1970.

Johann Heinrich Pestalozzi

- Jedan, Dieter., "Theory and Practice: Johann Heinrich Pestalozzi." Vitae Scholasticae,1990.

- Biber, George. *Henry Pestalozzi and His Plan of Education.* London: John Souter School Library, 1831.

- Silber, Kate. *Pestalozzi: The Man and His Work.* London: Routledge and Kegan Paul, 1960.

- Chisholm, Hugh, ed. *"Pestalozzi, Johann Heinrich".* Encyclopedia Britannica 11th Edition. Cambridge University Press (1911).

Bibliography

Carlson, Gregory C. *Understanding Teaching: Effective Bible Teaching* for the 21st Century. Wheaton, IL: Evangelical Training Association, 2005.

Fawcett, Cheryl. *Understanding People: Ministry To All Stages of Life.* Wheaton, IL: Evangelical Training Association, 2001.

Gangel, Kenneth O. *24 Ways to Improve Your Teaching.* Wheaton, IL: Victor Books, 1986.

Gregory, John Milton. *The Seven Laws of Teaching.* Grand Rapids, MI: Baker Books, 1954, 1975.

Hakes, J. Edward. *An Introduction to Evangelical Christian Education.* Chicago: Moody Press, 1970.

Meier, Paul D., et al. *Introduction to Psychology and Counseling.* Grand Rapids, MI: Baker, 2004.

Ormrod, Jeanne Ellis. *Essentials of Educational Psychology.* Upper Saddle River, NJ: Pearson Merrill Prentice Hall, 2006.

Powell, Russell A., Diane G. Symbaluk, and P. Lynne Honey. *Introduction to Learning and Behavior (Third Edition).* Stamford, CT: Wadsworth Cengage Learning, 2008.

Richards, Lawrence O., and Gary J. Bredfeldt. *Creative Bible Teaching.* Chicago: Moody Press, 1970, 1998.

Riggs, Ken. *They Call Me Doc.* Ashland, KY: FWB Publications, 2011.

Segall, Marshall H., et al. *Human Behavior in Global Perspective: An Introduction to Cross Cultural Psychology (Second Edition).* Boston: Allyn and Bacon, 1999.

Schultz, Glen. *Kingdom Education (Second Edition).* Nashville, TN: LifeWay Christian Resources, 2002.

Thigpen, Jonathan N. *Teaching Techniques: Revitalizing Methodology.* Wheaton, IL: Evangelical Training Association, 2003.

Towns, Elmer L. *How To Create and Present High-Impact Bible Studies.* Nashville, TN: Broadman & Holman Publishers, 1998.

Yount, William R. *Created To Learn.* Nashville, TN: Broadman & Holman Publishers, 1996.

Weiten, Wayne, et al. *Psychology Applied to Modern Life: Adjustment in the 21st Century.* Stamford, CT: Wadsworth Cengage Learning, 2006.

Whitaker, Todd and Beth Whitaker. *What Great Teachers Do Differently: 14 Things That Matter Most (Study Guide).* Larchmont, NY: Eye On Education, 2006.

Wong, Harry K. and Rosemary T. Wong. *The First Days of School: How To Be An Effective Teacher.* Mountain View, CA: Harry K. Wong Publications, Inc., 2001.

Biographical Information

Dr. Ken Riggs has been an ordained minister and educator since 1963. He has a broad background in many areas of ministry and education:

Ministry:
- Principal: First established Christian School in the Free Will Baptist denomination (1966-1969)
- Evangelist (1969-1971)
- Faculty: Free Will Baptist Bible College, teacher education, Nashville, TN (1971-1993)
- Adjunct Professor: Nashville State Community College, Nashville, TN (1992-present)
- Senior Pastor: West Meade Fellowship, Nashville, TN (1993-2003)
- Minister of Adult Education: The Donelson Fellowship, Nashville, TN (2003-2004)
- Administrator: Pleasant View Christian School, Pleasant View, TN (2004-2010)
- Interim Coordinator, Psychology Department: Welch College (formerly Free Will Baptist Bible College), Nashville, TN (2011-present)

Author:
- Books: *By The Way; They Call Me Doc*
- Booklets: *The Runaway, How To Live Right, You Can Know*
- Gospel Tracts: *Rather Fight Than Switch, Four Letter Words*

Workshop Leader:
- Family seminars and Sunday School Teacher Training
- Tennessee Association of Christian Schools teacher training conferences

Contributing Writer:
- *Contact* and *ONE* magazine

Education:
- High school diploma, Cohn High School, Nashville, TN (1959)
- B.A., Free Will Baptist Bible College, Nashville, TN (1964)
- M.S., Old Dominion University, Norfolk, VA (1971)

- M.Ed., Middle Tennessee State University, Murfreesboro, TN, (1973)
- Ph.D., George Peabody College For Teachers at Vanderbilt University, Nashville, TN (1978)

Dr. Riggs and his wife of 50 years, Carolyn, have three sons and ten grandchildren. They live in Nashville, Tennessee.

Made in the USA
Coppell, TX
07 December 2022

88086032R00066